A PAW PARTNERSHIP

A PAW PARTNERSHIP

HOW THE VETERINARY INDUSTRY
IS POISED TO TRANSFORM
OVER THE NEXT DECADE

NEHA TANEJA

NEW DEGREE PRESS
COPYRIGHT © 2020 NEHA TANEJA
All rights reserved.

A PAW PARTNERSHIP
How the Veterinary Industry Is Poised to Transform over the Next Decade

ISBN	978-1-63676-610-2	*Paperback*
	978-1-63676-679-9	*Hardback*
	978-1-63676-276-0	*Kindle Ebook*
	978-1-63676-277-7	*Ebook*

DEDICATION

I dedicate this book to my true soulmates and forever companions, my three German Shepherds: Heidi, Simba, and Leo. They inspired me to become the best leader I could be and a pet health advocate in aspiration of preserving the human-animal bond. The love I have for my dogs and my pet patients throughout the years has made my dedication to them grow, leading to the development of this book.

To my parents, Deepti and Vijay, my sisters, Reema and Mahima, and my husband, Sunny. Thank you for always encouraging and supporting me through all of my endeavors. You have always encouraged me to pursue my passion and put my best foot forward. You have shown me how to care for others. You've led me on the path of believing in others and supporting them even when they may not believe in themselves. Taking those with great potential under our wings and helping them chase their dreams turns out to be a life-changing experience that significantly humbles you. You have taught me unconditional love and selflessness.

To the pet patients and teams I have worked with throughout my career in veterinary medicine. You have inspired me to adopt a progressive way of thinking and explore ways on how to improve our future. You have solidified the importance of a team and how together we can make a bigger impact in the lives of our pet patients and each other. The past and the present lay the foundation for the new heights we can achieve and pave the way to our future.

CONTENTS

INTRODUCTION		9

PART 1.   **THE HUMANIZATION OF PET CARE**   **23**
CHAPTER 1.   MY FIRST PET   25
CHAPTER 2.   THE ROLE OF EACH TEAM MEMBER   35
CHAPTER 3.   THE TECHNOLOGY OF VETERINARY MEDICINE   53

PART 2.   **THE REAL-WORLD EXPERIENCES OF VETERINARY PROFESSIONALS**   **69**
CHAPTER 4.   THE PEOPLE OF PET CARE   71
CHAPTER 5.   THE REALITY OF PET CARE   85
CHAPTER 6.   BRIDGE THE GAP   103

PART 3.   **ADAPTING TO CHANGE**   **117**
CHAPTER 7.   CREATING A POSITIVE MINDSET   119
CHAPTER 8.   TOOLS FOR VETERINARY PROFESSIONALS   131
CHAPTER 9.   ORGANIZING PROCESSES   145

PART 4.   **PET CARE 2.0**   **159**
CHAPTER 10.   A VETERINARY PRACTICE IN 2030   161
CHAPTER 11.   THE EMOTIONAL WELL-BEING OF PETS   177
CHAPTER 12.   THE FUTURE OF PET OWNERSHIP   187

ACKNOWLEDGMENTS   201
APPENDIX   207

INTRODUCTION

"Bailey, Bailey stay with me girl." Her eyes fluttered, barely staying open, and her heart beat a mile a minute. Bailey, a mixed breed adult dog, came rushing in on a stretcher, with wounds to her face and blood dripping from her back legs. Dr. Jackson immediately called Mike and I to help stabilize her. We established an airway, hooked her up to monitoring devices, and started manual ventilation and chest compressions. Bailey wasn't going to survive. She was hit by a car, and the impact to her body was more severe than she could handle. She fought hard and took her last breath a few moments after she arrived. Her owner insisted we keep trying until the rest of her family could say goodbye. We continued CPR, in the hope a miracle would happen, and to ensure Bailey's family could see her one last time. These little miracles were what we hoped for even when the odds were slim. Dr. Jackson taught us to never give up.

I was barely eighteen when Bailey came in, with my entire career ahead of me. At the time, I didn't know what I wanted or how my future looked until I got my foot in the door. I had no idea how my passion for a part-time summer job would lead to a lifelong career. Bailey's case was one of the first emergency cases I assisted with while working in a small animal practice. All the skills I learned clicked at that moment.

Medical and technical skills weren't the only skills I needed to succeed in this profession. I learned the value of professionalism, compassion, and teamwork. I also learned that staying focused during a crisis requires immense concentration. They were skills I would use every day. For example, I had to maintain a calm demeanor and focus on trying to keep Bailey alive while providing support to her family who lost their best friend and companion. I knew that the time for processing loss wasn't there when I needed it. The emotional toll Bailey's death had on me would catch up with me several hours later. Until then, I had to push through the day with a smile on my face and continue delivering outstanding care for the next pet and client.

Over the past decade, I've seen many conscious attempts to change the culture in small practices and focus it on the pet's health and excellent customer service. But what happens when an employee loses a family member and calls out? How do we adapt when an employee submits a resignation letter? How do we respond when an upset client erupts at the reception desk at the very moment a patient emergency occurs in the treatment room? What happens when an overbooked appointment schedule interferes with our ability to train a new employee on the systems and processes of the clinic?

Because of Bailey, I began a path filled with unique emotional turmoil and its own industry-specific challenges. Not only have I learned the skills necessary to survive as a pet health professional, but I've also observed the factors that often contribute to my colleagues' successes and failures.

I've learned that it takes more than skill to combat the challenges of this field. We thrive as individuals when we share a commitment to one another and to establishing the grounds of a high-functioning team. We aren't there yet. But we can get there if we can overcome these industry-wide challenges: turnover, burnout, compassion fatigue, and poor work-life balance.

COMMON MISPERCEPTIONS ABOUT THE VETERINARY PROFESSION

Many misperceptions exist about the veterinary industry. One of the most common I have heard revolves around the notion that veterinarians aren't real doctors.[1] Au contraire! Veterinarians attend a four-year college and complete pre-veterinary school, as well as attend a four-year veterinary medicine program. Thereafter, the governing board of veterinary medicine requires state licensure to practice as a veterinarian. Additionally, veterinarians treat multiple animal species and learn about the body systems of large animals, small animals, exotic pets, reptiles, and more. Veterinarians receive schooling to build their knowledge in various areas of medicine ranging from general practice to surgery and specialty, making them experts in the field.

---

1   Mary H. Kramer, "Veterinary Career Myths," *The Balance Careers*, June 25, 2019.

I have also found many people think veterinarians make a substantial amount of money.[2] Veterinarians receive a base salary, and many are given the option to earn commission. This model causes stress for all veterinarians, but especially new grads and younger veterinarians who work extended hours to obtain advanced clinical experience. As a result, they have to make a choice of either supporting their financial situation or furthering clinic experience. Vets struggle to pay enormous student loans along with their other financial responsibilities. As of 2019, veterinarians accumulate an average of $167,534 in student loan debt, with the top 20 percent owing more than $200,000. As of February 2020, the average annual salary for a full-time veterinarian, working in a hospital, is approximately $73,000 for a recent graduate and $95,000 for a veterinarian with more than one year of working experience.[3]

Lastly, I have found that people think a day in the life of a veterinary team consists of an abundance of heartwarming experiences because they see puppies and kittens every day. In reality, there are serious challenges. Like many jobs, there are good and bad days. The assumption that veterinary teams experience high levels of job satisfaction is far from accurate. Yes, veterinary teams do treat puppies and kittens, but many of those puppies and kittens die. Nearly every day, a veterinarian delivers heartbreaking news to a family losing a loved one. Several times per week, the veterinarian along

---

2 Mary H. Kramer, "Veterinary Career Myths," *The Balance Careers*, June 25, 2019.
3 Melissa Horton, "Average Student Loan Debt for Veterinarians," *Lendedu*, November 27, 2019.

with the assistance of a technician or assistant euthanizes an animal in pain.

Veterinarians often care for patients their entire lives and frequently care for multiple generations of pets from the same family. Seeing pets from their first hellos to their final goodbyes wears on the staff. These long, intimate relationships take a toll on the professionals. After so many years of seeing the same animals with recurring problems, seeing terminal diseases take beloved patients, and long hours of demanding emotional requirements every day of the week, vets and animal care professionals experience compassion, fatigue, and burnout. Many professionals who experience compassion, fatigue, and burnout leave the profession, become quickly irritable, and spread that negativity across other team members. Some even stop practicing altogether or commit suicide.

THE PROBLEM WITH MISPERCEPTIONS

Veterinary medicine exhausts those in the field, emotionally and physically. For example, most of our patients don't have pet insurance, and when they're unwell, they can't speak to tell us what is wrong. Patient advocacy, therefore, falls on the veterinary staff—which includes the veterinarian, veterinary assistants and technicians, customer care representatives, and hospital managers, as well as the grooming and kennel teams. More than seventy thousand veterinarians in the US face job challenges that lead to disproportionately high suicide rates, according to the US Centers for Disease Control and Prevention (CDC). A CDC study published in January 2019 shows that veterinarians have the second highest suicide rate, compared to other professions, with male veterinarians 2.1 times more likely and female veterinarians 3.5 times more likely to commit suicide compared to the general population.[4]

These trends ripple out to other roles within the profession, with veterinary technicians also at risk. According to an article published in the *Annual Review of Psychology*,

> Veterinary professionals are exposed to raw emotions day in and day out. On top of witnessing the suffering of patients and the grief of clients, we have other stressors in our profession that contribute to burnout. A demographic study, conducted in 2016 by the National Association of Veterinary Technicians in America (NAVTA), confirmed that the number one reason why veterinary technicians leave the field is insufficient pay. This is followed by lack of respect from the employer (20 percent), burnout (14 percent), lack of benefits, childcare difficulties, lack of respect for the profession, and compassion fatigue. This has led to the suicide rate for veterinary technicians to be 5 times more likely for male technicians, and 2.3 times more likely for female technicians.[5]

Veterinarians frequently find themselves euthanizing a pet with a treatable injury or illness because the pet owner can't

---

4   Melissa Horton, "Average Student Loan Debt for Veterinarians," *Lendedu*, November 27, 2019.
5   Melissa Chan, "Veterinarians Face Unique Issues That Make Suicide One of the Profession's Big Worries," *Time*, September 12, 2019.

afford the remedy, which might include costly surgeries. For the compassionate individuals who tend to enter the field of veterinary medicine that's a heavy burden to carry on their conscience.

"You can say you're going to be stoic and put it out of your mind and say it's part of being a veterinarian," says McCauley, a pet parent to a dog, a cat, and a pig, "but the reality is over time, that weighs on you."[6] In her 2020 Ted Talk, Dr. Melanie Bowden addressed the deadly trend, as well. "We have a problem within our industry where more veterinarians are leaving the field than coming in. Five percent of veterinarians commit suicide."[7] Suicide has become an epidemic plaguing the profession and clearly shows that a high percentage of veterinarians are not experiencing job satisfaction in addition to the financial burden they carry.

MY RESPONSIBILITY TO BRING AWARENESS TO THE VETERINARY INDUSTRY

Having worked in the veterinary field since 2008, I have a diverse and well-rounded perspective of the challenges and obstacles veterinary employees and employers face. I feel called to bring awareness and support to the profession. Each member of the veterinary team has chosen their job because they care for animals and people. We love our pet patients and want to provide the best care for them.

---

6   Mary H. Kramer, "Veterinary Career Myths," *The Balance Careers*, June 25, 2019.
7   *TED*, "Melanie Bowden: What Being a Veterinarian Really Takes," March 10, 2020, video, 19:04.

In 2008, as a high school graduate, I joined a veterinary practice and worked my way up through many positions in the clinic and the company. I started in an entry-level position as a kennel attendant. My curiosity as to how the veterinary team treated their patients led me on a path driven by passion but fueled by determination to reach my professional goals and help animals and people.

Several years later, my role evolved into that of hospital manager. From that vantage point, I could see endless possibilities to improve our standards for managing and leading a practice. I learned to coach my team, build on individual strengths and weaknesses through collaboration, and leverage skills in a way that moved our team forward. I learned how to interact and build relationships with customers and clients.

Through each step of my personal development journey, I came to realize that few people outside our industry have an awareness of the blood, sweat, and—indeed—tears that go into working in this profession. But what I failed to realize was the amount of stress I, too, experienced in the workplace and that I, too, was at the point of burnout. One of the most difficult career decisions I've ever had to make was to step down as the leader and mentor for my staff and step back from my role as a veterinary practice manager and strategic planning coach. But that's exactly what I did in 2019. I prioritized caring for myself for a while, and I began to explore opportunities to continue my professional growth, which was at a standstill. This time "off" gave me a chance to absorb and process the experiences I had encountered in my veterinary career.

What commonalities existed across the board, and how could we improve them? How could I influence the future of the veterinary industry to focus on the well-being of not just the patients but of the health professionals? I encountered the same concerns in multiple practices across the country, even around the world, in my quest to research and develop this book. Veterinarians, support staff, and key industry leaders are aware of the challenges the industry faces, and together they're innovating solutions.

THE VETERINARY AND PET CARE INDUSTRY IS POISED TO TRANSFORM OVER THE NEXT DECADE

Veterinarians and their support staff routinely sacrifice personal time and well-being to care for their patients. As a community, we must recognize and celebrate the positive impact of our colleagues' work. When we fail to understand the demands and contributions of each role within our clinic environments, we may perpetuate the increasingly common sentiment among veterinary professionals who often feel undervalued, underpaid, and underappreciated. Fortunately, we can change that.

Transparency about job roles, clarity about job demands, and having compassion for the profession and each other can go a long way in building the foundation of the veterinary profession. Providing veterinary professionals with a network to lean on, as well as promote their well-being, can make a tremendous impact in helping professionals feel supported in the industry. The majority of professionals who work in the industry do so because they genuinely care about animals and have a passion for them.

Like me, many veterinary professionals have faced challenges, some have even left the industry due to the increasing demands of the workplace. Veterinary professionals deserve to be heard and recognized for how much they sacrifice and all the hats they wear. By setting boundaries, we can manage the demands of the workplace.

According to Stephanie Stephens,

> "It's a boundaries issue," says Dr. Bander. "Doctors also are not always so good at reaching out for help. That's routinely discouraged historically within our culture, when in fact they need help as any other human would with physical, emotional, and spiritual issues. Instead of going home to the spouse and children, they may stay with a patient even though that may not change the course of things. Then when they get home, it's hard to 'be there' physically and emotionally." Dr. Drummond says this mentality isn't really so unusual, since we were trained to practice clinical medicine. "Along the way we are conditioned to be a workaholic, superhero, emotion-free, Lone Ranger."[8]

Currently, many veterinarians and support staff feel they have to accommodate walk-ins and sick patients, and squeeze in all they can even when a reasonable amount of time to work up a case isn't available. Setting boundaries and restrictions around appointments, building space into the schedule ahead of time for sick appointments, and limiting the

---

8   Stephanie Stephens, "Compassion Fatigue: 3 Steps to Setting Boundaries in Healthcare," *Health eCareers*, November 15, 2016.

number of drop offs, surgeries, and new client appointments would prove beneficial in setting boundaries and restrictions around the schedule. By doing so, the veterinary team could perform a comprehensive workup of the incoming cases and thoroughly communicate follow-up care recommendations, which doesn't always happen now.

Another method that would prove beneficial in decreasing the demands of the workplace would be setting the expectation up front of what clients can expect. In 2020, COVID-19 amplified the bottlenecks and inefficiencies present in veterinary healthcare systems across the world. Reported wait times increased, appointment schedules booked up a few days and even weeks out, and the chances of obtaining a same-day appointment were slim. The entire structure of processes used pre-COVID needs revamping to streamline patient care and ensure the continuity of care. Practice professionals need to think outside of the box, revisit how to conduct basic appointments, and enhance their communication with clients and each other.

Veterinary medicine closely compares to human medicine in a number of ways. Where it differs, it differs greatly. Unlike human healthcare fields, little effort has been made to provide transparency into the personal sacrifice and emotional hazards innate to working in the profession. The reality of the job involves more than the act of helping sick pets become healthy again, although those ideal outcomes help sustain us as vet professionals on days when little else does. We must highlight both the professional challenges and personal demands to move forward as a profession and foster a brighter and more fulfilling future.

WHO IS THIS BOOK FOR?

This book provides an insider's look into the veterinary profession. Anyone who loves animals, especially if you are a current or future pet owner, will learn a lot about how the industry operates. Current and future veterinary professionals will benefit from reading about the transparency offered in this book around the challenges, various job roles, and what to expect when working in the profession. Anyone considering a career in veterinary medicine can benefit from reading this book, and truly understand what the industry is about. Future veterinary professionals have the power to positively impact the future of the industry.

Many veterinary professionals don't know what to do when they've hit a wall in their career. They begin questioning their decision to enter the industry. My goals are to help current veterinary professionals rediscover their purpose, educate new professionals on all that it takes to survive in this industry, and educate pet owners on how they can support veterinary professionals. This is the book I wish I had, the book I hope other industry professionals will also want to read to examine these challenging situations and consider how to overcome them.

WHY READ IT?

The professionals discussed in this book began their journeys invigorated by a passion for the industry. We'll find that each of them discovers how the very real challenges within this profession have affected their lives. There will be life-changing stories you've never heard before. Through the candid conversations, readers will catch a rare glimpse behind the scenes and gain valuable insight into the veterinary industry's operations and challenges. Finally, this book will help you understand how to overcome the challenges by discussing helpful tools for industry success and how to shape the future of the industry. The next time you meet or interact with a veterinary professional you will have newfound love, respect, and appreciation for what each and every one of these individuals does to make sure your pet lives a long, healthy life.

Pet care is a triad between pets, pet owners, and pet healthcare providers. How can we empower veterinary professionals to provide the best care for their patients and guide pet owners to make conscious decisions for their pets? Veterinary medicine is a forthcoming and progressive industry, but it needs to implement better systems and practices to ensure safeguards surrounding the mental health of the hardworking people who see this as their career and not solely a job. As a profession, we need to stop bandaging the issues facing our industry and, instead, commit ourselves to treating them holistically.

PART 1

THE HUMANIZATION OF PET CARE

CHAPTER 1

MY FIRST PET

When I saw her, I lost my breath. I absolutely couldn't believe my eyes. She vomited in the car on the ride home, and, being only twelve years old, I was thrilled even to clean up her vomit in my dad's car. I went to tell my sister, barely able to formulate the words while gasping "Daddy... brought home a PUPPY!" She didn't believe me. At this time in our lives, computer games consumed a good chunk of time, and she thought I tried to trick her out of the computer game. I said, "No, there's really a puppy in the garage, come see!" My sister came with me to meet our puppy, and we stared in awe. Our youngest sister came down after coloring in her books and screamed with joy, "We have a puppy!"

Our persistent begging and convincing conversations with our dad—for what seemed like the majority of our young lives—had finally paid off. Months before he brought her home to us, Dad took my sisters and I to meet a litter of about ten German Shepherd puppies. They ran around and showed off their energy and three little girls fell in love. Our favorite of the litter stood out as the most rambunctious and the only one with her big ears standing straight up. She was the one. When we went home without her that day, my little heart was broken. But now, Heidi the German Shepherd was ours, and our lives would never be the same.

Puppies, it turned out, need supplies. My family had no idea what type of supplies, and we had no idea there would be so many choices. Our first trip to the pet store overwhelmed us, but store employees knew what Heidi needed and helped us pick out just the right food, treats, and toys. They also shared information about a local dog trainer who held classes at their store. Our rowdy puppy definitely needed that. The trainer had needs too. She needed to see Heidi's vaccination records. My sister and I looked at each other, confused. *Vaccine records? There's a doctor for dogs?* We'd never heard that dogs needed vaccines and preventative care just like us. We had a lot to learn about being pet owners.

MEET THE VETERINARIAN

We made a trip to the vet's office, where a very nice lady greeted us with crayons and coloring books. We colored while Heidi waited for her appointment. A veterinary assistant called us into the exam room and asked us questions—like where she'd come from, what we fed her, and what she was like at home. "She loves to chew on furniture," I told the vet assistant, "and on Mom's shoes, but only one shoe from each pair."

After the vet assistant took Heidi's history, the veterinarian came into the room. He did a full checkup for Heidi. He educated us on what being a pet owner entailed. He talked to us about her diet and nutrition requirements, discussed the vaccinations she needed, and recommended having her spayed when she was six months old. He even gave us some tips and tricks on how to manage her puppy behaviors as she was teething. Her early life consisted of frequent vet visits, every two-to-three weeks for the first several months, and we spent a lot of time at the vet's office while she grew. We knew we had landed in good hands when the vet took the time to explain to us all of the care that our new pup needed. The most memorable time of our lives started then, and Dr. Jackson understood the importance of her role in our lives and welcomed her into his clinic family.

Shortly after Dr. Jackson finished his exam, the vet assistant took Heidi to the treatment room for her vaccines. I kept peeking through the window that led to the back of the clinic. I wondered, "What happens back there?" As Heidi grew, my curiosity about that back room grew, too. Every time we took her to the vet's office, someone in medical scrubs would disappear with her into the secretive back room. *Someday, I'm going to go find out what they do in there.*

THE BEGINNING OF MY VETERINARY CAREER

Now let's fast forward a couple years to high school. During my senior year of high school, each student sought out a worksite and mentor to conduct a three-week internship as a requirement for graduation. The guidelines instructed students to find a worksite where we could observe how an industry functioned, as well as gain hands-on experience. Growing up, I dreamt of a career as a professional basketball player, then an animal cop, after watching so many episodes of *Animal Precinct* on Animal Planet.

The veterinary clinic piqued my curiosity since day one. So, by default, during Heidi's next vet appointment I asked the veterinarian if I could work with him to fulfill the internship requirement in May of my graduating year. With a big smile, and so much enthusiasm, Dr. Jackson said, "Why yes of course! We'd be happy to have you here and help you in any way we can." I was thrilled! Now I could finally find out what happened with Heidi when she went to the back for her medical treatments and her grooming-related needs.

I spent the first couple of days meeting team members and shadowing the doctor. He took me into appointments with him and gave me homework on medical conditions or diseases that were discovered during the day. While Dr. Jackson caught up on his phone calls and medical records, I worked with the technical staff and saw how they treated pets.

Some days consisted of surgical procedures and professional dental cleanings, all of which underwent anesthesia. I remember the lead technician, Sharyl, asking, "You won't pass out if you see blood, right? I want to make sure to catch you if you do like one of the other students did." She chuckled along, and I said, "Nope, I've got this!" I surprised myself! The thought of needles scared me growing up, and I thought the procedures conducted in a medical facility would gross me out. Funny enough, the complete opposite happened, and my interest in the industry sparked, helping me overcome my fear of blood and gore.

After spending some time with the technical team, the client service team members showed me how they processed appointments, made follow-up and reminder calls, and performed the tedious tasks that had to be completed in preparation for upcoming appointments, procedures, and boarding drop-offs over several days. At this time, one of the customer service representatives, Denise, encouraged me to fill out an application. As summer concluded, they were frequently hiring as the seasonal staff returned to class. At this time with college right around the corner, the possibility of having my first job hadn't crossed my mind. Luckily, I decided to stay local and filled out my first employment application.

What an eye-opening experience to see all the different people working in the clinic, the types of cases they saw throughout the day, and the dynamic between the medical staff and the administrative staff. Each group had a vital role in ensuring smooth operation of the clinic. If anything broke or didn't follow the guided process, this directly impacted the lives of the patients. In my short time as an intern, I gained so much valuable insight about the industry and continued growing from there.

Summertime came to an end, and I called Jay, the clinic manager, to follow up on my application. He invited me in for an interview, and as the following Monday came around, I dressed in my business casual attire and arrived with a resume in hand. My nerves kicked in, and I proceeded into the clinic for my interview. When I arrived, Jay shook my hand and asked, "Can you start on Tuesday? You're hired." The smile on my face, and the excitement of landing my first job, reinforced my love for animals. A dream of working with puppies and kittens all day slowly manifested its way into reality. I immediately replied and said, "Yes! I can!" I had to give him my class schedule, but luckily it worked out. The clinic was just a short walk from my college campus, and I could work part-time while completing my bachelor's degree.

My first day came, and it didn't begin as I had expected. The facility I worked at had an array of services they offered, one of which was a boarding facility for dogs and cats who stayed while their owners traveled or were away. Of course, this was my first job, and I hadn't had prior experience with company and business protocols. As I got used to working and going to school, I developed a routine—and started building a career in this industry. My first year, I learned a few lessons that would never leave me.

LESSONS LEARNED

LESSON #1—DAY TO DAY LESSONS/SKILLS
When I started off as a kennel attendant, my shift started in the morning by making rounds of the boarders, cleaning out their cages, providing them with fresh food and water, administering medications, washing the dishes, mopping the kennels, and restocking items in the clinic to prepare for the remainder of the day. Learning about food, cleanliness, and sanitation are foundational skills no matter which job you take. These day-to-day lessons formed my thought process around the importance of making sure each pet received adequate amounts of food, monitoring their appetite, thirst, elimination behaviors, and overall attitude. As time went

on, I slowly started assisting with restraining patients for treatments.

As a new industry professional, I did a lot of housekeeping and taking care of the boarded pets, as well as cleaning. I learned how to use a *real* mop at the clinic for the first time. I mean, Swiffer classified as the new generation mop. Using a mop that slides on the handle, has to be changed daily or in between possibly contagious cases, and a separate one for surgery was so new to me. Mop heads are typically reused, rewashed, and replaced. At the time, I didn't know that. The first time I took out the mop, I forgot to wring it out, and the Licensed Veterinary Technician (LVT) couldn't help but crack up. Understanding this was my first job, she kindly showed me how to use the mop. At home our primary method of mopping involved a cool Swiffer Jet.

LESSON #2—NOBODY GETS HURT
Transitioning into my role as a veterinary assistant, I learned the importance of properly holding a pet for the veterinary technician. My job focused on making sure the pet couldn't bite or scratch the other person by maintaining control of the patient, as well as ensuring the way I restrained didn't cause the patient discomfort. Some patients cooperated without a fight. Others presented as very stressed and fearful, so we had to adjust how we handled them. Teamwork was the name of the game. Recognizing a team members' work ethic and handling procedures, and how it complemented mine, determined the safe handling of the pet. In the past few years, fear-free practices have become more commonplace. More to come on the emotional well-being of pets in Chapter 11.

LESSON #3—NONVERBAL CUES

Boy, that was a lot of pressure. How do you prevent an animal from biting or scratching while administering vaccinations, drawing blood, taking x-rays, and more? Our patients couldn't tell us if they were in pain, their fear level, or what they felt. The veterinary team interpreted and picked up on nonverbal signals. Nonverbal communication, in the form of cues and signals, allowed the team to learn so much about canine and feline body language and oftentimes the ability to read these signals determined the outcome of the visit.

Many people think that an overactive and hyper dog in a veterinary practice is excited. Behind the excitement is fear, anxiety, and stress (FAS), which are important for not only veterinary professionals but also pet owners to understand to ensure the patient has a pleasant experience throughout their visit. For example, approaching a dog from the front is perceived by the dog as a threat, and many dogs react. The best way to approach a dog is to let the dog approach you, don't make eye contact, and approach from the side. A slow but gentle approach will allow the dog to become comfortable with you. Nonverbal signals from dogs that indicate when a pet is relaxed come in the form of a soft, loose mouth, normal pupils, wagging tail, and a flexible posture. A stressed dog looks very different. The lips are pulled back, pupils dilated, the ears alert, the posture rigid, tail tucked, and the mouth closed with a snarl or bite in the works.[9]

---

9 Fear Free Pets, LLC, "Fear Free Certification Program," Module 1 Fear Free Behavior Modification Basics at Fear Free, LLC, accessed May 8, 2020, https://fearfreepets.com/courses/fear-free-certification-program/#l1-introduction.

Similarly, cats are extremely fearful in new locations and meeting them head-on is confrontational. When approaching a cat, let the cat come out of the carrier on its own and fill the general space with pheromones and treats to make it more comfortable. The fear-free practice certification serves as a great tool for veterinary professionals and pet owners to learn about the dos and don'ts of how to interact with a pet. It is geared toward veterinary practices but may also prove beneficial for pet owners. Nonverbal cues from cats vary from that of dogs. Normal pupils, ears forward, rear end higher than the shoulders, the tail straight up or with a slight curve, and a closed mouth indicate a relaxed cat. In contrast, when the pupils are large and round, the ears face the side or back, crouched body, legs tucked, tail curled or whipping, and hissing, panting, or an open mouth presents the cat is stressed.[10]

LESSON #4—THE PHYSICALITY OF THE JOB

In a small animal practice, we saw a variety of kittens, cats, puppies, dogs both big and small, and some of them bigger than me! Some dragged me through the parking lot when I tried to collect a urine sample. I thought to myself, if I planned on staying in this profession for the long haul, I needed to start lifting weights at the gym. As time went on, it definitely built up my self-confidence to show off the small biceps I started building. The other assistants and technicians would encourage me and my colleagues to continue with our body-building efforts. This made a *huge* difference. Getting strong enough to more easily handle patients for treatments while the more

---

10   Fear Free Pets, LLC, "Fear Free Certification Program."

experienced staff performed the necessary treatments made the days much easier on my body. I didn't expect how strenuous and taxing the physicality of the job would be coming into the profession. The job requires physical strength, in combination with working long shifts on your feet all day.

TO SUM UP THE LESSONS LEARNED

Who would've expected the job and all of the intricate details about learning how your teammates function, how pets communicate, and the physicality of the job would be so intense? Caring for a living creature brought so much joy and knowledge. Helping a helpless pet and providing compassionate care became part of me. Being able to see microscopic findings on a pet and being able to treat the patient as directed by the veterinarian were important demands of the job. These skills allowed me to provide better care for my own pets as well and motivated me to continue educating myself and learning about veterinary medicine.

As I gained more experience, my curiosity grew, and I had many questions. I started to wonder about the industry professionals who came before me. How did veterinary medicine evolve into an essential profession? Who first developed these skills and techniques? How did the medical industry for animals come about? As I continued to work in the field, I realized many of the clinic roles consisted of transferable knowledge. Many of the lessons and skills I learned related to pieces of jobs influenced by other industries—accounting, maintenance, insurance and billing. I wondered how this all got to where it is now.

CHAPTER 2

THE ROLE OF EACH TEAM MEMBER

The 2003 release of the Humanization of Pets Study marked a pivotal moment for every segment of the pet products and services industries. The study's findings would quickly revolutionize not only the way pet products were developed, designed, packaged, and branded, but also which products and services would be developed. And the innovation was only beginning.

In 2011, Americans aged fifty-five to sixty-four spent an average of $636 per year, the most on their pets of any age group. "In addition, homeowners spent $653 on average, compared to renters, at $221. With baby boomers entering retirement and a housing recovery in place, that may mean the population willing to spend big on their animals is about to grow."[11]

---

[11] "An Era of Change: A Closer Look at Veterinary Education and Practice," *University of California*, 2015.

Pet owners were evolving, and their relationships with their pets looked much different than they had a decade before. The new breed of pet parents, as many prefer to be called, humanized their pets, caring for them and providing for them much the way they would a human child. By default, medical care for animals became more prominent, and pet parents' expectations for the level of care reflected pets' status within their households and, indeed, within their family structure.

Today, pets are more loved and cared for than ever before. Food and veterinary visits made up the top categories for expenditure for pet owners, with this number on the rise. According to a recent pet owner survey by *Statista*, as of March 2020, over sixty-three million households in the United States owned at least one dog, making them the most widely-owned type of pet across the US at this time. A total of 42.7 million households owned cats, as the second most common pet to own, with freshwater fish in third place. As a result, 67 percent of households own a pet in the United States, with birds and horses coming up as the next most commonly owned pets.[12]

Seventy percent of pet-owning households comprise of millennials, making this cohort the largest group of pet owners in the US. Not only do millennials love their pets, but they're also more likely to have a pet than have a child. According to City Journal, "Americans spent seventy billion dollars in 2018 caring for and feeding pets; they spent fifty-nine billion

---

[12] Emma Bedford, "Number of Pet Owning Households in the United States in 2019/20, by Species (in Millions)," *Statista*, March 24, 2020.

dollars on childcare."[13] Evidence suggests that the greater the bond between a pet owner and their fur baby, the higher the level of veterinary service expenditures, when finances can support them. However, even when limited financial resources exist, some owners choose to go into debt to provide veterinary care for their pets.[14]

Pet health care is dominated by teams of veterinary professionals across a variety of clinics and hospitals. In this chapter, I review the roles of the healthcare team members in the veterinary profession, and how each professional plays a vital role in the care of a pet and the client. Many veterinary team members not only work as providers for their four-legged patients, but also function as therapists and mediators for their clients and colleagues. You will come across a familiar theme throughout this book, about the importance of relationships and how they carry on from one person to the next. The relationships built in the veterinary community go a long way, and many of those people become part of each other's families.

ROLES IN THE VETERINARY PROFESSION

Hospital operations depend on the team in the hospital. Each team member has a crucial role in ensuring the mission of veterinary medicine is adhered to and patient care is provided in the most humane way. In the veterinary profession,

---

13   Michael Hendrix, "Are Cities Going to the Dogs?" *City Journal*, October 8, 2019.
14   "An Era of Change: A Closer Look at Veterinary Education and Practice," *University of California*, 2015.

there are two prominent avenues in which veterinary professionals are employed. I will focus on those employed in corporate and private level practices. Private and corporate level practices have similar hospital level roles. However, in a corporate level practice, the positions extend out to higher levels of management, executive and director level roles both clinical and nonclinical.

The day-to-day routine of a hospital employee is anything but routine. No day starts the same way as the one before, and each day presents a different set of challenges. A veterinary team usually sees a wide variety of cases on a daily basis, from routine preventative care appointments to sick appointments, surgeries, dental cleanings, and emergency cases. From my observations, the average ratio of veterinary assistants per doctor consists of two assistants or technicians per one full-time equivalent (FTE) doctor. From my experience, the ratio increases in highly functioning practices to three or four assistants or technicians per FTE. Employees of veterinary practices with a higher ratio of assistants or technicians per doctor appear to have higher levels of job satisfaction, productivity, camaraderie, and develop a loyal clientele.

Whether a veterinary practice is privately owned or part of a larger corporation, the job titles of its employees looks relatively similar. Typical vet clinics have:

- Customer Service Representative(s)/Receptionist(s)
- Groomer
- Kennel Assistant(s)
- Veterinary Assistant(s) (VA)
- Licensed Veterinary Technician(s) (LVT)

- Practice/Hospital Manager(s) (PM/HM)
- Veterinarian(s) (DVM/VMD)

Since each role in the office is responsible for maintaining their own area of jurisdiction to keep the well-oiled machine running, let's examine each briefly.

CUSTOMER SERVICE REPRESENTATIVE / RECEPTIONIST (CSR)

From the moment a client and pet patient enter the front door, front desk reception staff attend to their needs. Behind the desk, the client can anticipate seeing Customer Service Representatives (CSR), Client Care Specialists (CCS), or Receptionists. CSR's perform essential duties similar to those performed by receptionists across any industry that requires customer interaction and quality service. Those duties may include:

- Greet clients and schedule appointments
- Educate clients on service offerings
- Read and review medical records
- Answer multiple phone lines and manage communications in person and via phone, text, and email
- Communicate patient status with the medical team
- Ensure clients understand pre-appointment preparations or restrictions
- Review estimates, billing, and discharge instructions with clients
- Triage appointments with the appointment schedule

An effective CSR should also have basic medical knowledge because the first person a client interacts with is a CSR. If the first impression of a veterinary clinic doesn't demonstrate the ability to triage a medical appointment, answer basic questions about vaccines and wellness, or effectively communicate the services an incoming pet may need, this can create discrepancy and questions about the quality of the hospital services.

GROOMER

A groomer is responsible for the physical care of a pet's coat and nails. To become a certified pet groomer, professional schooling and a certificate of completion are required. The tools groomers use to care for a pet require extensive training and care to maintain the coat without causing injury to themselves or the pet.

The primary duties of a groomer consist of:

- Bathing services
- Haircuts
- Shampoo, condition, and blow-dries
- Nail trims
- Non-medical ear cleanings
- Schedule future grooming appointments
- Learn to recognize abnormalities of the skin, hair, coat, paws, ears, and teeth
- Communicate with the veterinary team about any abnormal findings

Some pets visit their groomers more frequently than they visit their veterinarians. Through the course of providing a pet's ongoing and frequent skin and coat care, a groomer naturally familiarizes herself with the pet's physical appearance. It's not uncommon, therefore, for an attentive groomer to be the first to notice changes or abnormalities in a pet's condition. I certainly owe my dogs' groomer a debt of gratitude. My dogs—Simba and Leo—see their veterinarian three or four times per year. They see their groomer, Masha, almost every month. So, when a hard mass appeared on Leo's left leg in 2018, Masha noticed. Because his groomer massages and cleans him, a mass the size of a dime grabbed her attention, she grabbed mine, and because of this relationship, our veterinarian successfully removed the mass before it spread.

Some veterinary facilities enjoy the luxury of having a groomer on staff. Not only does the on-site grooming service provide a one-stop-shopping convenience for the pet parent, it can also reduce stress on the pet. The positive relationship groomers build with a pet can ease the visit for the pet as a veterinary patient, and the frequent grooming visits can help the pet form a positive association with the clinic facility itself. When the grooming and veterinary healthcare staff can work together to tailor the visit and experience to the pet, the result is comprehensive, head-to-tail pet care.

KENNEL ASSISTANT

Veterinary offices also offer boarding services in addition to grooming and medical services. Boarding facilities in a medical practice are especially helpful for patients who require special attention, administration of medications via oral administration or an injection, or monitoring of a medical condition, for example a diabetic cat or a pet who recently had a surgical procedure. A lead veterinary assistant or technician usually supervises the care of boarding patients, but the kennel assistant remains responsible for the primary care of a boarding patient. The basic duties of a kennel assistant are as follows:

- Feed animals, walk dogs, clean up housing
- Monitor changes in health: appetite, elimination habits, stress level, comfort, cleanliness
- Update assistants, technicians, and doctors on the status of pets with medical conditions
- Maintain hospital cleanliness
- Rotate laundry
- Perform basic pet restraint and handling
- Stock the hospital with essential, everyday supplies

A kennel assistant is a vital part of the veterinary team because they provide care for the patients who are boarding. As an entry level kennel assistant progresses, they have the opportunity to grow into the role of a veterinary assistant or veterinary technician through the appropriate training and potentially completing the required degree to obtain a license to practice as a veterinary technician or veterinarian.

VETERINARY ASSISTANT (VA)

The title of a Veterinary Assistant is very broad when it comes to all of the hats a veterinary assistant wears. This group of professionals begin their training many times as a kennel assistant and progress into the role of a VA. Step one usually consists of learning to read the nonverbal cues and signals given off by the patients and recognizing the common signs and stressors for patients. A veterinary assistant typically assists with the hands-on care of patients and is responsible for an array of duties, as listed below (may vary based on state laws):

- Triage appointments
- Educate clients on a variety of preventative care and disease processes
- Administer vaccinations, monitor anesthesia, take x-rays of various body cavities and extremities
- Perform professional dental cleanings under anesthesia
- Collect and prepare lab samples for collection ranging from blood, urine, and fecal collection, to cytology and fungal cultures
- Assist and prepare in surgery, maintain and sterilize surgical equipment, and assist in CPR
- Perform basic grooming needs: baths, nail trims, ear cleaning, anal gland expressions, sanitary shave, and so on
- Fill medications as prescribed by a veterinarian
- Review estimates and treatment plans with clients
- Assist with training of new hires by functioning as mentors

A veterinary assistant functions almost as a para-doctor and leads the treatment of the cases a doctor works up. Veterinary assistants ensure the delivery of patient status updates, recommendations, and anything else related to the patients' medical care via phone calls, informational handouts, emails, and personal contact. Many veterinary assistants also volunteer their time for other duties, such as ordering supplies for the hospital, participating in marketing and community outreach events, and many choose to become a certified, or licensed veterinary technician.

LICENSED VETERINARY TECHNICIAN (LVT)

A licensed veterinary technician is often looked upon as the leader of the technical team. To obtain licensure, the individual is required to attend a two-year program, and completes an associate degree in Veterinary Technology. There are a variety of in-person, online, and hybrid programs that allow students to work and attend school at the same time. Upon completing the schooling requirements, studying for the Veterinary Technician National Exam (VTNE) begins. Preparing for the exam is no less than any other board exam and requires months of intense studying to pass. The Board of Veterinary Medicine requires veterinary technicians seeking licensure to complete a three-hour, 170 multiple choice question exam to become licensed. The exam takes place through three different cycles during the year and examines applicants on many different subjects studied throughout the program.

Having personally completed this schooling to become a licensed veterinary technician, I can attest to the value of gaining experience in the industry prior to completing the degree program. Typical coursework in a veterinary technician program consists of focused courses about the science of multiple species and performing externships consisting of six hundred in-clinic hours. Becoming an LVT requires hard work, but at times the effort put into completing the requirements for licensure goes overlooked due to the deficit of LVT's across the profession. As a result, many hospital teams must leverage their staff to ensure the upkeep and maintenance of patient care standards.

Licensed veterinary technicians perform all of the duties of a veterinary assistant, in addition to the following (may vary based on state laws):

- Place IV catheters and endotracheal tubes
- Administer IV anesthesia and sedation
- Monitor hospital stock of controlled substances under supervision of a licensed veterinarian
- Perform cystocentesis to obtain a sterile urine sample
- Maintain licensure by completing continuing education credits as determined by the state he or she is licensed in
- Train, develop, and mentor colleagues

For those seeking a veterinary career, I would strongly recommend gaining working experience while going to school or prior to enrolling in courses. The material presented in the courses will become more applicable as it's learned, giving students a complete picture versus little tidbits. Applying knowledge as you go has much more value than having to figure out how to apply it at a later time.

As of September 2020, the Board of Veterinary Medicine was working on highlighting the role of LVT's by potentially changing their title to better align with all of their duties, which line up with those of human nurses. Many veterinary technicians seek greater acknowledgment surrounding their job roles and request a title more fitting of their job duties. I believe this is a step in the right direction to empower individuals in the field and give them credit for the work they do.

A title similar to that of a human nurse better aligns with and provides greater understanding around all that a veterinary technician does in a veterinary hospital.

PRACTICE/HOSPITAL MANAGER (PM/HM)

Through the chain of command, the most experienced and highest positioned team member is the leader and practice, or hospital, manager. LVTs, individuals with or without industry experience, or those who have exemplified they have the ability to lead a hospital qualify as candidates for the practice manager position. The practice manager is usually a high performing employee who has earned the trust and respect of their peers in the hospital or someone new coming in.

Personally leading a hospital and a team signified one of the greatest achievements and milestones in my career. I knew I wanted to make a difference in the lives of my team, the pets, and the clients. With the determination and guidance from my previous manager, Jay, I embraced my new position. I remembered him saying, "This is your hospital now. Make sure you adopt an ownership mentality and lead this hospital as your own baby." I never forgot his words. I had to make sure my team was happy. Their welfare depended on how I decided to run the hospital, as well as navigate interactions between other team members, to create a cohesive, collaborative environment where people functioned as a team rather than a high school drama.

The duties of a practice manager are endless, requiring more than forty-hour work weeks, with no overtime pay. The average work week of a hospital manager ranged anywhere from fifty to sixty hours per week. If an employee called out from a shift or the schedule was overbooked, the manager had to figure out how to fill the gaps, oftentimes resulting in the practice manager working late on the floor or setting up interviews to hire new employees. The responsibilities of a hospital manager entail the entirety of all hospital operations including, but not limited to:

- Produce financial results
- Motivate the team
- Implement training standards
- Create hospital protocols
- Ensure all hospital maintenance is up to date, including building and equipment
- Provide a structured workplace where people can come together to work toward a common goal
- Provide excellent client service and experiences
- Market and build relationships with community partners
- Conduct performance reviews
- Manage human resources
- Maintain supply chain levels
- Attend meetings, which require travel throughout the year
- Monitor payroll
- Monitor the financial health of a practice by evaluating profit and loss statements

Managers must build a solid relationship with the medical director or veterinarian in charge. The practice manager and medical director function as a unit that the entire team looks up to for guidance. They work together to meet the expectations of each other, their peers, and upper management on how the hospital should perform.

VETERINARIAN (DVM/VMD)

In conjunction with the hospital manager, the veterinarian plays a critical leadership role in veterinary practices. They are constantly being watched by their team members and colleagues, have very little down time, and oftentimes don't have the luxury of taking a break during their long shifts. The busy work schedules easily amount to over fifty hours per work week. Most employees look to the veterinarian for direction regarding patient care. Veterinarians are required to hold the appropriate license to practice and are expected to know all of the body systems of multiple animal species. The duties of a veterinarian in a small animal general practice include, but are not limited to:

- Perform routine and emergency surgery
- Conduct outpatient procedures
- See patient drop offs
- Offer wellness care
- Educate on nutrition
- Euthanize patients
- Build client relationships

Veterinarians act as nutritionists, internal medicine specialists, surgeons, dentists, emergency physicians, pharmacists, phlebotomist's, mentors, and grief and anxiety counselors for their clients and team members. Certainly, like any doctor, they're expected to have a good "bedside manner" when speaking with pet owners. Pet owners bring with them all of their emotions and attachments to their animals, and vets must be prepared and have the soft skills to navigate such conversations with people. In this way, veterinarians really function as counselors for their patient families and team members, while trying to practice medicine. It isn't uncommon in veterinary practices where close working relationships are formed, and members of the team provide emotional support for one another.

Veterinarians also oftentimes work as "relief" veterinarians, which means they fill in shifts for clinics on an as needed basis instead of working for the clinic as a permanent team member. A relief veterinarian has more independence when it comes to their schedule and usually receives pay for an hourly rate regardless of the number of cases they see.

SETTING EXPECTATIONS

When entering the profession or deciding to go to school to become a veterinarian or licensed technician, all of the demands of the job may not be obvious. The profession is very rewarding but also very taxing on an individual and understanding the requirements of the job can help alleviate any preconceived notions.

As an enthusiastic newbie, the profession feels enriching and exciting, but it's also important to understand the realistic demands. Some days are full of seeing puppies and kittens, but not without a fair share of cleaning up diarrhea, vomit, or being peed on. As a common experience for many who enter the industry, some decide this is where they want to be, whereas others do a trial period and decide it isn't the right profession for them. The trial period really contributes to burnout. Someone might believe they belong in this profession but after a few months or years into it, they decide against it and change course. So now, the person whom we invested time and energy into training leaves with no replacement in site.

A typical shift never goes as scheduled. More often than not, employees stay longer than their scheduled shifts, sometimes without a break. As a "retail-healthcare industry," we have to serve our clients and sometimes that happens at the expense of employee wellness. This isn't how it should be, but the profession has evolved as such that client retention and customer satisfaction have preceded employee wellness, and it has to transform for the well-being of the people in pet care. Having reasonable expectations of the job and the profession is crucial to avoid some of the challenges our profession faces today. For example, burnout and compassion fatigue, which I will discuss further in Part 2 of this book.

As I spent more years in the profession and my knowledge base grew, my team began to rely on me more, and the services that we could offer to clients began changing. Educating a pet owner about basic vaccinations became educating pet owners about early disease detection and preventative dental cleanings. This then evolved to communicating doctor treatment plans and lab follow ups and even more client education. All of the mental effort required in the midst of a hectic schedule and a salary that didn't allow me to live the life I wanted for myself and my family made me question if it was worth it.

Is the stress, job responsibility, and struggle to create a personal life worth it? No one goes into veterinary medicine to become a millionaire, but there should be enough balance to allow individuals to build a life they dream of while doing a job they love. Building a strong foundation and understanding about the industry allows for greater perspective around how it operates. The next chapter goes into the history of veterinary medicine and the evolution of technology in the veterinary space.

CHAPTER 3

THE TECHNOLOGY OF VETERINARY MEDICINE

"Neha, I need you to develop these x-rays now." My supervisor handed me a cassette, then rushed off to see another patient, pausing just long enough to add, "Don't mess up, this is a fractious cat and we only have one chance."

I took the cassette with the x-ray film inside the dark room, a tiny six-foot by three-foot room. Behind the x-ray machine, a filing cabinet had extra film, extra cassettes, and the developer machine. I went into the dark room, closed the door behind me and ran the x-ray through the processing machine. Just as the film reached completion, the door cracked open a few seconds too early. I almost cried. The head technician told me to make sure this one film was developed because McQuain wouldn't tolerate another x-ray, but the door opened. How did the door open?

I left the dark room and took the x-ray to my supervisor and told her what happened. As the last words left my mouth, I started squinting my eyes in anticipation of her reaction. Some smoke left her ears, but she gently told said, "Alright, well let's try again and see if he'll cooperate." Luckily McQuain's patience hadn't been fully expended and he tolerated another x-ray. The day of digital radiology couldn't come soon enough!

Manually developing x-rays, taking pet patient measurements, and setting the exposure levels of the machine based on the measurements took extra time, patience, and people. A few years later, the clinic received the gift of digital radiography and a few bonus items. The technique chart included the numbers that should be set on the x-ray machine to ensure appropriate exposure levels versus manually measuring a pet to determine the machine settings. In addition, a computerized machine displayed the x-ray instantly and allowed users to design the order the x-rays should be taken in.

With the older machines, veterinary technicians would set the view to be taken on the machine, stop before the next image was shot to change the cassette and set the x-ray to the next body part and so on. Production of quality x-rays and sharing them with pet parents enlightened the process and allowed for them to be sent to board-certified radiologists with a turnaround time of twenty-four hours or less. This phenomenal integration of upgraded technology allowed for the entire veterinary team to experience more flexibility when taking x-rays because less time had to be spent through the manual process.

THE HISTORY OF VETERINARY MEDICINE

Digital radiology is one of thousands of advancements in veterinary medicine throughout its history. The earliest known evidence of the practice of treating the health of animals exists on ancient rolls of paper. The Kahun Papyrus of Egypt captured the first written accounts of veterinary medicine dating back to 1900 BCE. The Kahun Papyrus of Egypt consists of two distinct writings that outlined the fields of human and animal medicine and the similarities between the two when it came to treating humans versus animals and vice versa. The Kahun Papyrus discusses animal gynecology, particularly that of cattle. These pieces of literature indicated that people began investigating animal medicine. A couple thousand years later, archaeologists discovered fragments of an ancient veterinary medical textbook that covered diseases related to birds, cattle, dogs, and fish. Horses were the primary focus of ancient medical care because of their economic importance for transportation, agriculture, and trade.[15]

In 1761, the first veterinary school opened by Claude Bourgelat in Lyon, France, which marked the beginning of veterinary medicine. The profession began in an effort to stop the plague that spread by infected cattle in France and England. The plague, also known as the Cattle Plague in the eighteenth century, infected several herds of cattle and took almost thirteen years to eradicate. Veterinary medicine began in an effort to investigate and fight off diseases carried by sheep, horses, and cattle. At that time, the primary function of animals focused

---

15 "Retrospective: A Brief History of Veterinary Medicine," *Oakland Veterinary Referral Services* (blog), September 27, 2019.

on agriculture, consumption, and war. To decrease the prevalence of disease in animals, decrease or eradicate zoonotic disease, and keep the agriculture industry alive, it became important to start investigating how zoonotic diseases spread and how to contain them if not eliminate them completely.

Claude Bourgelat loved horses, which sparked his interest in animal medicine. He fought to make his case on the importance of veterinary science. Bourgelat wrote on veterinary science, which helped him gain traction and recognition. In one of his books, *Elements of the Principles of Veterinary Art, or, New Knowledge About Medicine and Horses*, he wrote: "Those who intend to [acquire skills in veterinary art] will not be able to acquire a sufficient degree of education ... [since] we do not have schools for teaching." This book helped him become a member of the Academy of Science in France.[16]

On August 4, 1761, King Louis XV's Royal Council of State finally granted him the authority to open the Royal Veterinary School. Bourgelat made his first steps. To maintain the credibility of this institution and prove the value of having a veterinary school, he published numerous results achieved by his students on fighting the Cattle Plague and other zoonotic diseases. Admission required that a student be able to read and write—without any other criterion. Many who already received training as doctors were automatically dismissed as veterinarians because Bourgelat feared those who enrolled in his school would leave veterinary medicine and focus solely on human medicine.

---

16   Malinda Larkin, "Pioneering a Profession: The Birth of Veterinary Education in the Age of Enlightenment," *JAVMA News*, (December 19, 2010).

As far as the teaching curriculum, Bourgelat believed students should have more exposure and experience than solely lecture. He created a teaching environment and hybrid classes that allowed students to take part in lecture but also supplemented them with weekly hands-on experience, primarily with cattle. Bourgelat decided to open a veterinary school at the right time, when the Cattle Plague hung heavy over Europe. This helped him prove the importance of veterinary medicine when it came to preserving public health, discovering answers about zoonotic disease, and caring for animals by investigating zoonotic disease that took a toll on Europe in the eighteenth century.[17]

HOW VETERINARY MEDICINE BEGAN TO EVOLVE

Eventually, veterinary medicine made its way to the United States of America. In 1852, the Veterinary College of Philadelphia opened as the first veterinary school in the United States. The Veterinary College of Philadelphia operated until 1866, and during this time the American Veterinary Medical Association (AVMA) was established in 1863. The AVMA serves as the leading advocate for the veterinary profession by protecting, promoting, and advancing the needs of veterinarians and their communities. Shortly thereafter, in 1884, the Bureau of Animal Industry under the USDA opened and remained in operation until 1900.

---

17   Malinda Larkin, "Pioneering a Profession: The Birth of Veterinary Education in the Age of Enlightenment," *JAVMA News*, (December 19, 2010).

Succeeding the Veterinary College of Philadelphia, in 1883, the School of Veterinary Medicine at the University of Pennsylvania (UPenn) came into establishment. UPenn, known as the oldest accredited veterinary school, still remains in operation. The purpose of the veterinary school at UPenn resulted in an effort to protect the public from infectious diseases through contaminated meat, eradicate diseases in animals, and improve the quality of livestock.[18] Additionally, in 1965, the Food and Drug Administration (FDA) added a Veterinary Medical Branch to oversee veterinary pharmaceuticals. It later became the Center for Veterinary Medicine (CVM), with a mission of "Protecting Human and Animal Health" and making sure an animal drug is safe and effective prior to releasing it to the market for pet health use. As medicine began to evolve, so did the types of animals that veterinarians treated. Companion pets became more integrated into the lives of humans in the nineteenth century. As people sought care for their pets, the technology used to treat, diagnose, and care for pets evolved to meet their needs.

THEN AND NOW

Technology continues to evolve and change, requiring additional talent, skill, and focus on these areas. Technology is part of the "growing pains" in growing a business, and as technology and medicine continue to evolve, so will the demands of the various positions in a hospital. The question of who will be responsible for ensuring that the industry can

---

18 L. Cole, "A Quick History of Veterinary Medicine," *Canidae* (blog), November 4, 2014.

keep up with the changing technology remains. One individual doesn't have enough bandwidth to look over every detail in a practice. The technology of medicine will require creating more specialized job roles to ensure that veterinary medicine continues to advance, without which we could experience increased stress and burnout in the industry.

From the 1900s, the technology of medicine dramatically evolved. The emerging technology, even since 2008, such as the internet, social media, smartphones, and education have advanced. Some of the major changes that have taken place over the recent years are:

Technology—Then and Now.

Then	Now
• Paper medical records • Microchip • Phone calls • In-clinic food and medication pick up • Film x-rays • Black/White ultrasounds • Invasive surgery • Treat sickness • Gas-induced anesthesia • Word of mouth • Yellow pages and simple websites • In-person education and how-to guides • Dial-up internet • Veterinarian • General Practice Veterinarian fulfilled all specialist roles	• Electronic medical records • Microchip with temperature control • Email, text message, live chat • Home delivery of veterinary supplies • Digital x-ray, MRI, and CT scans • Advanced computer-generated ultrasound with color • Laparoscopic surgery • Prevent illness through routine preventative care • IV anesthesia • Social media • Interactive websites • Videos • Internet • Dr. Google • Board-certified specialists • Educational platforms • Apps for smartphones • Constant contact • DNA test for pets • In-house laboratory machines

Back in 2008, my clinic team consisted of fifteen employees to maintain paper medical records, conduct treatment, assist in surgery, and triage appointments. Now we expect the same number of personnel to also manage social media networks, websites, multiple avenues of incoming and outgoing communication via email, phone, and text message, and to respond to requests immediately. These expectations present insurmountable challenges for veterinary teams.

The human medical industry adapted to this wave of change about five years ago with many providers converting to electronic medical records, email, and text communications. Increasingly more physicians and nurses recorded patient histories on laptops or tablets during patient visits. Data entry is much more robust, accurate, and less time-consuming. The consistency in record-keeping, as doctors and staff are able to type up medical records, continues to improve instead of depending on interpreting handwritten records.

Maintaining, learning, and adapting to the new technology comes as an uphill battle for the veterinary industry. One example of the impact of technology lies in the migration of paper medical records to electronic. In 2015, I led the practice I managed through an electronic medical record (EMR) conversion, as well as numerous other veterinary practices. As medical record management improves, many believe the quality of care has also. Well-written medical records allow for more fluid communication and continuous care because the records are legible, consistent, and follow a formatted layout. A common issue with an EMR conversion across multiple hospitals always falls back on the training of staff on how to use the medical record management system.

A few lucky people championed the new software and quickly became the point of contact for the team. The implementation of training programs initially existed and were mandated, but the availability of time and payroll dollars dwindled over time. Management expected new hires to perform their job duties without the time to learn new software. As a result, veterinary practices struggled to keep up with emerging technology.

MARKET DEMANDS

As veterinary medicine continues to evolve, market demands continue to change as well. To stay in step with the advances in veterinary health care, hospitals must develop and execute strategies consistent with current market demands. The retail industry developed and shared five strategies employed in hospitals today to meet the rising demands of health care. According to Gamble, the five most significant strategies employed by human hospitals are "to emphasize convenience, identify and meet distinct local market needs, be proactive in patient outreach, adopt a customer opportunity perspective, and disrupt the notion of 'patient loyalty.'"[19] This section discusses three of the five principles.

Molly Gamble interviewed CEO John R. Thomas of MedSynergies for her article "Five Retail Principles for a More Effective Hospital Market Share Strategy." He believes that instead of focusing on "what should be done," medical providers

---

19   Molly Gamble, "5 Retail Principles for a More Effective Hospital Market Share Strategy," *Becker's Hospital Review*, April 3, 2013

should shift their focus to thinking about "what their patients need."[20] This method allows for greater patient satisfaction. Gamble mentioned emphasizing convenience as the first strategy. For example, by making veterinary care more accessible and convenient for pet patients, the time in between requesting a test and receiving the results decreases. As a result, a time savings occurs for the client in between visits and treatment, which is more convenient for the pet and the pet owner. This leaves the veterinary industry with happier clients and more effective measures of practicing medicine.

However, with convenience comes a price. Many people work eight hours per day, five days per week, but in the veterinary industry many practices stay open past six o'clock in the evening. Those working in the industry have families, friends, and lives apart from work that need balancing. Will urgent care centers become more commonplace? Will the veterinary industry always operate on an extended schedule, or could creative scheduling alleviate the stress of achieving work-life balance while catering to the pet owner population?

Another example of increased convenience for a patient is having access to all of the services and equipment in one location. This allows the treatment of a pet's medical condition to take place in one facility, in a familiar location, and with familiar people. For example, many veterinary clinics offer boarding, grooming, training, surgery, dentistry, and radiology in their practices allowing for more comprehensive care of the pet patient.

---

20 Molly Gamble, "5 Retail Principles for a More Effective Hospital Market Share Strategy," *Becker's Hospital Review*, April 3, 2013

The second strategy, "being proactive in-patient outreach," involves marketing, customer service, and being knowledgeable about the demographics of the pet population. Familiarity with the population allows for veterinary hospitals to gain useful knowledge about the demands and needs of their pet patients and allows hospitals to offer better customer service. With focus on customer service, the level of customer satisfaction will increase, and in turn, the reputation and growth of hospitals will flourish. This allows for future success of the hospital and separation of good clinics from bad.

The next strategy says that providers shouldn't assume that their clients will remain loyal to them because there may be better providers out there, "disrupting the notion of client loyalty." Stable clientele provide comfort for veterinary hospitals because it reduces the possibility of clients leaving and going to another provider. Staying ahead of the curve, building relationships, and focusing on maintaining a loyal customer base helps ensure veterinary practices build trust with their clientele and allows for the continuity of pet care. One method my clinic used to build client and employee relationships was by sending out cards to clients for milestone events, vacations, and feel good things. Receiving an unexpected card helped build and maintain the clinic relationship with the client and employee by exemplifying we cared about not just the pet, but also the people.

The top strategies employed vary among veterinary hospitals, but, based on my research, veterinary hospitals should utilize these three strategies discussed above. By assessing market demands, patient needs, and submarkets most hospitals remain competitive. As long as veterinary teams pay attention to the changing demands of veterinary health care and take it upon themselves to change with the market, veterinary professionals will continue to grow and remain in business. The development and institution of new medical practices when it comes to preventative care, treatment, and diagnostics determines future hospital successes. If veterinary hospitals continue to focus on their patients, client education, and building a strong team, the foundation of the hospital becomes a pillar to future success.

SPECIALISTS

Increasingly, veterinarians and veterinary technicians choose to advance their education by specializing in certain areas of veterinary medicine. Consequently, there have been many changes in how veterinary practices operate. Many veterinarians make recommendations for pets to see specialists, but not everyone can afford specialized care for their pet. A pet parent shared with me her personal experience when her dog Baxter's illness presented. Baxter's condition slowly deteriorated, and the vet recommended additional testing to determine the cause of his discomfort. Baxter's owner upgraded his wellness package at Banfield to do more diagnostic testing. However, when the vet determined Baxter likely had a bladder tumor and needed to see an oncologist, the owner didn't know what to do. He was twelve years old, but the initial consultation, additional exams, and chemotherapy treatments amounted to over $10,000 with not many financial resources or insurance options to help her pay for Baxter's treatment.

Many pet owners aren't prepared for emergency situations that may occur with their pets, but not many feel there is enough financial support to allow them to care for their pets beyond what can be done at a general practice. Baxter's owner had no additional resources other than to make him comfortable while the cancer slowly debilitated his body.

On the other side of the spectrum, the veterinarian who wants to prolong the life of the pet is unable to treat the condition in a general practice and seeks a referral to a specialist. Dr. Coleman shares that most people have no idea that there are cardiologists for pets, and thinks now we're at a point where specialized care benefits the pet's health. Educating pet owners about how veterinary medicine has evolved, the technology available to provide advanced care, and insurance options saves pet owners and veterinary professionals a lot of emotional trauma and financial burden down the road.

TECH-SAVVY PROFESSIONALS

Medical specialists play a critical role in specialized care for pets. Subsequently, I'll share with you the importance of specialized roles from an operational standpoint. At the beginning of this chapter, I laid out the changes in technology from 2008 to 2020. As a veterinary professional, specifically a practice manager, the requirement to keep up with evolving technology comes with a full training package but limited time for completion. The roles of veterinary professionals changed from being solely veterinary healthcare providers to multi-talented professionals with tech-savvy skills, social media gurus, and professionals adept in written communication.

It feels like new technology emerged overnight, but many industry professionals, especially those in the veterinary space, haven't received proper training and support to keep up with the advances in technology. The gravity of difference between written communication and verbal communication and how the receiver interprets it leads to many instances of miscommunication and altered perceptions. When the intention to deliver a professional message via text message comes across as rude or abrupt, the message relayed falls apart in the delivery. Many long-term industry professionals used telephones or in-person contact as the primary methods of communication and now struggle with typing on a computer; whereas the younger generation grew up with smartphones and lack the skills to communicate face-to-face or hold verbal conversations like people once used to.

The technology of medicine, evolving market demands, and specialized care have culminated into the perfect storm for the veterinary industry. The general population has more access to care and convenience, and those in the profession need to stay above water to keep up with the evolving demands. The newer generations of pet owners are smarter and faster than ever when it comes to using technology, developing apps, tracking services, and using technologically advanced devices.

As technology continues to advance, the gap between the care provided by veterinary teams and the staff's ability to use and learn evolving technology will limit the level of care offered. To begin to close this gap, hospitals and educational institutions should consider providing courses on how to survive in a technologically savvy healthcare industry. Updating requirements of potential employees and requiring those entering the profession to have a level of understanding when it comes to using advanced technology will help stay ahead of the curve. Advanced technology use for medical procedures, record-keeping, and client communication is crucial for the future of veterinary medicine. Courses on how to deliver written communication in a professional yet clear manner require further refinement, focus, and training from all hospital personnel involved to ensure effective communication between hospital staff and clients.

To achieve a technologically savvy workforce, veterinary professionals should invest time in learning about technological advances in veterinary medicine. Specialized personnel can assist with maintaining hospital operations and train staff to use new technology. By doing so, veterinary professionals can keep up with the influx of new technology and pair it with what they already know. Technology has inserted itself into veterinary medicine, and it's here to stay.

PART 2

THE REAL-WORLD EXPERIENCES OF VETERINARY PROFESSIONALS

CHAPTER 4

THE PEOPLE OF PET CARE

―

I was thrown in, sink or swim. I was expected to know things that I hadn't been taught. Training was not an option; you figured it out along the way. It's true that being thrown into veterinary medicine gave me strength, perseverance, and character. However, it also allowed me to make a TON of mistakes. In addition, it gave me nights driving home, wondering if I should leave the field all together. Fourteen years later, I realized that "sink or swim" is not the way to start with a new employee. If you want your employees to be successful, you can't set them up for failure.

—JADE VELAZQUEZ, LVT.[21]

---

21 Jade Velazquez, "How Can You Improve Mentorship in Your Clinic?" *Dr. Andy Roark*, March 3, 2016.

Creating a productive, pet-first atmosphere requires effort. In my career as a veterinary professional, I've been fortunate enough to work in pet-first environments with an awareness of how our work directly impacts pet outcomes. An atmosphere as such depends on the structure, framework, and culture built within a veterinary practice and team. By focusing on a shared goal—something larger than each of us as individuals—we could navigate workplace politics in a constructive manner, rather than allow them to bog us down. Veterinary clinics that fail to cultivate this type of environment may instead foster one that's quite at odds with the sensibilities of their employees. Veterinary professionals experience an immense amount of stress due to their caseloads. If they don't have the framework to manage stress or have healthy habits in place to help them work through difficult situations, burnout in the profession continues.

For veterinary professionals to continue providing advanced care, as a community we need to take a step back and understand the various components of the job and all the sacrifices veterinary professionals make. The people of pet care have unpredictable daily schedules, work later than their scheduled shifts, and work weekends, weeknights, and holidays. As a result, rescheduling or cancelling plans with family or friends isn't uncommon. Veterinary professionals spend 80 percent of the workday on their feet and sometimes don't have time to take a break. They also attend to after-hours calls and critical cases. Veterinary teams offer this availability because of the relationship built between them, the client, and the pet.

Veterinary teams work hard to provide pet care but often struggle when it comes to hiring, training, and retaining employees. To start off, practices focused on training and development have the ability to cultivate a culture of associate mentorship, which many industry professionals seek. Most of us in the veterinary space embody an array of similar traits. Individuals drawn to this field are compassionate, empathetic, have a desire to give, and an eagerness to learn. These traits serve as positive attributes to possess and have potential to develop through professional guidance in the veterinary field.

STATISTICS

Several thousands of veterinary practices and veterinary professionals exist in the United States. The veterinary industry comprises 66.6 percent of companion animal medicine, with the remaining 33.4 percent in large animal, the food industry, and other sectors of pet care. The table below outlines a breakdown of the statistical findings related to the number of professionals, the average salary, average age, and percent of females who work as veterinarians, veterinary technicians, veterinary assistants, and other veterinary professionals:

Statistical Findings for Veterinary Professionals.

	Veterinarian[22]	Veterinary Technician[23]	Veterinary Assistant[24]	Veterinary Professionals[25]
Number (count)	89,200	112,900	99,500	402,000
Average Salary ($)	95,460	35,320	28,590	45,661
Average Age (years)	44.5	33.7	33.7	36.5
Female (%)	64.9	90	90	83.4

All of the above-mentioned professionals provide service to eighty-five million pet owning families in the United States.[26]

On average, a male veterinarian practices as a vet for twenty-four years, but a female vet only practices for sixteen years of her career. Additionally, a veterinary technician or assistant spends an average of seven years in practice. The amount of time veterinary professionals spend in the industry alarms me. The discovery of these statistics made me realize we need

---

22 US Bureau of Labor Statistics, *Veterinarians: Occupational Outlook Handbook*, (Washington, DC, last modified September 1, 2020).
23 US Bureau of Labor Statistics, *Veterinary Technologists and Technicians: Occupational Outlook Handbook*, (Washington, DC, April 10, 2020).
24 US Bureau of Labor Statistics, *Occupational Employment Statistics*, (Washington, DC, July 6, 2020).
25 "Data USA: Veterinarians & Veterinary Technologists and Technicians." Data USA, accessed April 12, 2020.
26 "Facts + Statistics: Pet Statistics," Insurance Information Institute, accessed September 3, 2020.

to do something about this and find a way to build the veterinary workforce.

What if it didn't have to be this way? What if the well-known veterinary associations and larger corporate companies provided more support and training on how to hire, train, and retain employees. What if veterinary practices created practice cultures that encompassed career growth plans as part of the employees' time within the company? Professionals seek mentorship, work-life balance, and a positive workplace that allows professional and personal growth.

IMPROVING THE HEALTH AND WELLNESS OF VETERINARY PROFESSIONALS

Better methods exist today that could greatly improve the health and wellness of industry professionals. Oftentimes experienced and inexperienced veterinary team members find themselves tasked with training new team members on how to perform basic care requirements for hospitalized patients and discuss the importance of preventative vaccinations and testing with clients. A senior employee, even with only one or two years of experience, frequently finds themself responsible for the training and development of new hires while performing their individual job responsibilities. Along with the support staff, veterinarians also assume the role of educating new employees to effectively leverage the team in the long run.

This type of situation creates a stressful work environment when dedicated time for training and development is scarce.

Utilizing already limited personnel resources to maintain in-clinic operations and then tasking them with cultivating a quality employee takes time. Establishing guidelines around how to hire and train veterinary staff and develop plans of how to retain the current workforce could prove beneficial in maintaining the integrity of veterinary teams and the care they deliver to their pet patients.

HIRING VETERINARY PROFESSIONALS

Vacancies in the veterinary world never end. Veterinary hospitals almost always have a position to fill, whether part-time, full-time, seasonal, or temporary. I strongly believe hiring managers would benefit from establishing a set of criteria when hiring and recruiting veterinary professionals. Hiring teams and managers should conduct interviews with the mentality of cultivating an irreplaceable, long-term employee and provide support for personal and professional growth.

Michelle, a former colleague of mine, works as a veterinary practice manager. She began her journey in the veterinary industry in 1993. Throughout her career she's worked in many different roles in various aspects of veterinary medicine. With all her years of experience, Michelle shared hers about hiring new employees. One employee in particular came to mind when I asked Michelle about her experience. She started off by telling her story about a difficult employee who was equivalent to "the cancer on the team."

> You know every time I try to catch this person so I can discipline them they straighten up long enough that I

can process them out. As a manager, it's really our job to protect the health of the team. So, if there's somebody not working out you get them off. Bad but true.

Michelle reached out to her boss for advice on how to deal with this difficult employee. Her boss guided her and said something to her that stuck even seventeen years later. He said,

> As long as you create the right environment, those people will find their way out. You're working hard, helping your team do the best they can, and everybody's doing the right thing. That person isn't going to fit. You're going to expect the same thing from them as you do the rest of the team. As a result they'll work their way out because they're not going to fit in with what's driving your team or align with the goals of the practice, and it will become obvious.

When hiring an individual for a practice level position, hiring managers ask themselves a series of questions.

- Will they perform all job duties with enthusiasm, even the mediocre tasks such as cleaning up vomit from a dog who ingested a toxic substance? (Not so pretty!)
- Will this person shy away from cleaning up bloody diarrhea, and only gravitate to the more attractive tasks such as drawing a blood sample?
- What's the capacity of this individual, and how much effort will they put in to prove they are the right fit for this position?

Many leadership teams struggle to find resources on how to conduct worthwhile interviews to bring out character traits in the interviewee. Hiring managers may not realize that recruiting employees requires networking and building relationships with people all year round, not only when a vacancy occurs. To conduct meaningful interviews, numerous resources exist on the worldwide web of how to hire the right candidate and what types of interview questions to ask. By asking the right questions, managers gain insight about a person's character and how they may handle certain situations with other team members, clients, and pets. The American Veterinary Medical Association (AVMA), Veterinary Practice News Magazine, and the Veterinary Hospital Managers Association (VHMA) provide preliminary guidance on how to hire the right candidate for a veterinary practice.

In addition, many methods to conduct interviews exist. Phone, in-person, and working interviews prove useful when searching for and evaluating applicants. As a practice manager, when I searched for new employees, I posted year-round vacancies and regularly interviewed candidates. When the time to fill a position came, I already had a pool of applicants to choose from. Last-minute scrambling to fill a vacancy in a veterinary hospital lasted months. I couldn't afford to lose this time because I was already short-staffed.

Waking up the next day and expecting to find the right candidate never happened. It required investing time early on to find someone who matched the practice culture, values, and philosophy. Proactively building a network and dedicating time to conduct thorough interviews and perform assessments eased the difficulty in filling vacancies. As a hiring manager, when you spend the time to do the leg work up front, the chance of finding quality candidates increases exponentially.

TRAINING PET CARE PROFESSIONALS

After hiring comes training. High school graduates make up a majority of the applicant pool for veterinary support staff positions, such as a receptionist, veterinary assistant, or a kennel assistant. High school graduates are among the most adaptable and trainable individuals, but they also recently started making adult decisions, taking responsibility for themselves, and figuring out what comes next. Will they pursue further education, gain work experience to make a career choice, or do both?

The majority of veterinary professionals entering the industry receive on-the-job training. However, with the current statistics mentioned earlier in this chapter, the average time a veterinary assistant or technician spends in the industry limits new hire training by experienced professionals, leading to inadequate professional development. When gaps exist in foundational knowledge, mistakes, errors, and mishaps occur at an exponentially higher rate. If training initiatives followed a plan, veterinary employees could all be on the same playing field. The gap between generations of employees and their knowledge base would reduce.

Everyday veterinary practices work on molding high school graduates into successful and professional employees. As a step, why can't school systems start educating students earlier on potential career options out of high school? Some school districts offer students the opportunity to enroll in an animal science course where students gain a glimpse of what pet care entails. Other school systems encourage students to seek out opportunities to gain insight into different professions, similar to what I did right before graduating high school. In fact, according to the US Bureau of Labor and Statistics, the rate of enrollment in a four-year college of high school graduates decreased from 69.1 percent to 66.2 percent from October 2018 to October 2019, with 37.8 percent of those enrolled in a four-year program actively working.[27]

At the core, training and development creates a sustainable framework in retaining employees. When it comes to building a knowledgeable and capable veterinary team, new industry professionals should explore veterinary assistant certification programs. Doing so better equips future veterinary professionals with a framework on which to build their skills and knowledge. On-the-job training will always exist, but certification will lead to a more wholesome experience and allow future veterinary team members to become part of a cohesive team.

RETENTION OF VETERINARY PROFESSIONALS

Jade Velazquez highlighted one of the major missing pieces in veterinary medicine, mentorship and training. These two topics aren't always formally discussed, but they are crucial when it comes to retaining employees and top talent.

---

27 US Bureau of Labor Statistics, *College Enrollment and Work Activity of Recent High School and College Graduates Summary*, (Washington, DC, last modified April 28, 2020).

When individuals have decided to continue a career in such a space, establishing a mentee/mentor relationship provides utmost value.

Jade shared in an interview with Dr. Andy Roark,

> I am surprised by how many clinics still throw new employees to the wolves. They put them into rooms, they allow them to talk to clients, and they allow them to work on patients. This all happens without providing any training, structure or support. After this "training" process, management or veteran team members complain about mistakes made. That isn't acceptable. It doesn't have to be like this. We all can play a role in changing the environment. Whether you're a doctor, technician, assistant, receptionist or kennel attendant, you have something to teach someone. You also have something to learn from someone else. Yes, many of us had to work hard for any knowledge we gained. But if we take time to share it, we can build up and empower newer generations to get that knowledge now![28]

Throughout my career as a veterinary professional, and specifically as a practice manager, I've interacted with numerous veterans and rookies in the profession. Some made major career changes and others have only ever worked in this profession. I witnessed how many people thought they wanted to become a veterinarian. This fascinated me. How

---

28 Jade Velazquez, "How Can You Improve Mentorship in Your Clinic?" *Dr. Andy Roark*, March 3, 2016.

does someone know they see themselves working at a veterinary clinic, never having stepped foot into one or having worked with animals? Shortly after a working interview, or a few weeks into the job, the same individuals decided they couldn't handle it.

On the contrary, professionals who entered the industry with love for animals and started in entry-level positions climbed mountains. They achieved one promotion after another and didn't settle. The high performers learned everything possible about veterinary care and the operations, but once they maximized on their career growth, the horizon looked slim. Many companies struggle to keep top talent and so do veterinary hospitals. Top performers exhibit a unique skillset, which doesn't always translate into what the next step in a veterinary organization may be. The higher ups, already overwhelmed with their list of tasks, find it difficult to empower, enlighten, and encourage top performers to continue to grow or provide positions where their skills can be used. As a result, the highly skilled and talented people leave for other opportunities that can capitalize on their skills and fuel their passion for growth.

That was me in 2019. Among the group of people who furthered their education and were extremely motivated, but it got to a point where no further opportunities or positions existed to continue my career growth. Those in director and VP level positions remained in them for years, and tenured employees continued to be internally promoted. I wanted to focus on enhancing patient care, improving processes within the system, and providing mentorship to other veterinary professionals.

There were no next steps in sight besides becoming a veterinarian. Dr. Van Sickle responded,

> That's really sad because why do you have to become a veterinarian to accomplish improving patient care? You shouldn't have to be a veterinarian to do that. In fact, if you became a veterinarian you probably wouldn't have time to accomplish this because you would be focused on seeing cases. Wouldn't it be nice to have more people on the veterinary team who aren't necessarily veterinarians but could focus on and specialize on how to improve the current industry? These people are just as crucial as the veterinarian!

Former Chief Economist of the AVMA, Michael Dicks provides some insight. Through his research, he has identified six major problems the industry must address for the veterinary profession to perform to the expectations of veterinarians and their clients:[29]

- Ethical stress surrounding treatment decisions
- Financial stress among associate veterinarians and practice owners alike
- Buy-out of veterinary practices by those motivated solely by profit
- Volatile labor markets
- Increasing barriers to patient care
- Lack of continuous data to help identify potential solutions[30]

---

29 Michael Dicks, "Fixing the Veterinary Profession before It's Too Late," *VIN News*, May 13, 2019.
30 Ibid.

These issues have persisted since at least 2000, yet no profession-wide effort to address them has occurred.[31]

Many technicians I've worked with who wanted to continue learning and growing in their careers ended up transferring to emergency or specialty practices where they saw a different caseload. This stimulated their continued interest in veterinary medicine, while equipping them with a different knowledge base than that of a general practice. The people of pet care feel overworked, undervalued, and underpaid. We need our voices heard, and a push for more understanding and compassion to combat the challenges that we face.

---

[31] Michael Dicks, "Fixing the Veterinary Profession before It's Too Late," *VIN News*, May 13, 2019.

CHAPTER 5

THE REALITY OF PET CARE

———

"Dr. Jackson, we have a critical case and she's not doing well."

In most workplaces, the workweek begins with pleasantries, such as, "What did you do this weekend?" Not in this workplace. Not on this day.

The veterinary technician's announcement had set Dr. Dave Jackson's morning in motion. As he rushed toward the treatment room, he heard the anguished wail of the pet owner. Everyone, it seemed, knew the pet's prognosis appeared grim.

The experienced veterinarian and his team battled the odds, determined to stabilize the gravely ill patient. Two more technicians entered the treatment room—one with the next patient in tow, the other with some charts under her arm. Three charts, to be exact, because three pet parents had just dropped off their three pets. With four patients now waiting in queue and a distressed pet parent anxiously awaiting an update, Dr. Jackson maintained his focus on the patient emergency. By the time his patient crashed, the remainder of the vet's day seemed impossible. And it was only 8:45 a.m.

Welcome to Monday morning in veterinary medicine.

On television, time stands still at the time of death. Lights dim. Distraught doctors and nurses pause to console and support each other. Someone in the room knows exactly what to say to comfort a team who fought to save a life—and lost. In Dr. Jackson's clinic, time seemed to have no mercy that day. On the other side of the exam room door, a patient and pet parent had been waiting for nearly an hour to see the vet. That pet owner knew nothing of Dr. Jackson's intense, hour-long attempt to save another client's beloved pet, and it was his job to protect his clients from the reality of another pet owner's pain. So, he did what we always did on mornings like this. He took a deep breath to compose himself, put on a smile, and opened the door.

"Hi! I'm so sorry for your wait. Let's take a look and see how Dahlia's recovering from her ear infection today."

A typical workday for a veterinarian and veterinary team often plays out like this. Already stretched thin and over-booked, veterinary teams don't have enough wiggle room to accommodate the unexpected. And in a pet hospital, the unexpected is the one thing you *can* expect. One patient's prescription *will* take longer to fill. Another patient's owner *will* arrive late. At least one patient *will* refuse to cooperate during his exam. Emergency walk-in patients *will* cause a backlog. A veterinarian *will* have to sit down with a concerned pet parent to discuss test results and treatment options. No matter how skilled or how dedicated these hardworking pet health professionals may be, a family *will* go home without the pet they've grown to love. And sometimes, a veterinarian will have to administer an injection to end a pet's untreatable suffering.

As a pet owner, however, when you're caught in the backlog on a day like this one, you're unaware of what's happening behind exam room doors and in the back rooms, off limits to all but clinic personnel. As you sit in the lobby with a sick or restless pet, you might even assume it's an ordinary day in the life of your veterinarian. And you'd be right.

Some days feel like there's no end in sight, and one thing keeps coming after another. The toll on the entire veterinary team during these situations feels insurmountable. Some days it feels like you're drowning, and there's no way out.

The people taking care of the pets don't always have the support and tools necessary to function in a healthy work environment. More often than not, many pet care providers become part of the growing crisis in veterinary medicine escalating burnout, compassion fatigue, depression, and suicide. A little bit of compassion goes a long way with these professionals. They see patients during appointments, procedures, drop-offs, and walk-ins, and on top of that they regularly train new team members because of the high rate of turnover. All of these factors contribute to an ongoing set of challenges veterinary practices face, and it's not sustainable.

JOB BURNOUT

According to the Mayo Clinic, "Job burnout [is] a special type of work-related stress—a state of physical or emotional exhaustion that also involves a sense of reduced accomplishment and loss of personal identity." Common risk factors of job burnout are listed below.[32]

- Identifying so strongly with work that you lack balance between work life and personal life
- Having a large workload, including overtime work
- Trying to play the role of everything to everyone
- Working in a helping profession, such as health care

Someone once told me that scheduling is an art. Scheduling patient appointments requires immense planning and preparation, without which chaos strikes. One of the most important components to alleviate the stress around the appointment book directly relates to the staff schedule. For example, if a clinic expects to see fifteen pet appointments but doesn't have the scheduled staff to support the incoming workload, employee stress exponentially rises. In addition, incorrect appointment scheduling and lack of communication between the clinic and the client leads to additional time spent reviewing recommended services during scheduled appointment times.

The stress around appointment schedules and staff schedules make the perfect recipe for job burnout. In between seeing

---

32 "Job Burnout: How to Spot It and Take Action," *Mayo Clinic*, November 21, 2018.

a busy appointment schedule, veterinarians and their support teams follow up with clients about lab results, future plans, doctor recommendations, and more. Many practices try to cushion appointment times with an additional couple minutes to perform call backs, but when complications in procedures arise or pets need extended exams for their medical issues, it becomes difficult to complete these tasks in between appointments.

The follow-up process typically includes a call back or email asking for an update on the pet, discussing abnormal lab result findings, reviewing recommended treatment options, and/or sharing supplemental client educational material. Abnormal lab results take anywhere from fifteen to thirty minutes or more to work up. On top of that, communicating the disease process to the client and developing a long-term plan requires a lot of mental effort and communication. Inconsistency in the process creates room for error and unhappy clients and employees. When stress kicks in, mistakes happen. Employees don't have time for a break, overtime hours incur, and we continue to roll in the same pattern of inefficiency, stress, and burnout.

In a March 2020 TED talk, Dr. Melanie Bowden shared a candid assessment of what it's like to be a veterinarian today:

> Going to veterinary school is one of worst financial decisions a person can make. I will be hundreds of thousands of dollars in debt when I graduate, and this is very typical. The average salary of a veterinarian equals about the same as a department store manager (and large animal vets can be half of that), so as you

can see it's a real struggle for most people to pay off that much debt with a comparably mediocre salary. If money was the driving factor for me, I would have gone into human medicine—which costs the same for schooling, but the payoff is over double that of vets. But I didn't. I'm expected to be a counselor, an educator, a financial advisor, a team leader. I am the face and reputation of our business. When we can't fit this impossible standard. When we can't possibly fit in one more pet without compromising the care of others or compromising the health and well-being of my team by making them safe.[33]

Dr. Destiny Coleman had similar experiences early in her career. Having graduated from the University of Pennsylvania in 2015, Dr. Coleman began her career in private practice. Eventually, she oversaw two general practices as the lead veterinarian. The practices she managed assisted lower- and middle-income families in providing care for their pets. Dr. Coleman shared with me the inconsistency in her work schedule from practice to practice, and how an overbooked schedule ultimately led to sacrificing the quality of medicine. Providing top-notch, quality care remains at the forefront for all veterinary professionals.

Dr. Coleman said,

> I'll tell you that at any hospital I've worked at it's never been predictable; you almost never get out on time.

---

[33] *TED*, "Melanie Bowden: What Being a Veterinarian Really Takes," March 10, 2020, video, 19:04.

You're overbooked with appointments, which means you might be sacrificing the quality of medicine or even your ability to communicate effectively. So, I personally think finding that target number of appointments one doctor should see in a day is important.

Change takes time, persistence, and perseverance. Change takes someone to look at a broken and repairable cycle, step in and push people to do what's uncomfortable and out of the norm. Change needs to take place to help the veterinary community succeed in the profession and fight the battle against job burnout.

COMPASSION FATIGUE

Another critical concern in the veterinary industry, compassion fatigue referred to as the "cost of caring" for others in emotional pain, takes a toll on industry professionals. "The work of helping requires professionals to open their hearts and minds to their clients and pet patients – unfortunately, this very process of empathy makes helpers vulnerable to the profound affects and even possible damage by their work."[34]

Veterinary workers as a whole, take a considerate approach when communicating with their clients and treating their patients. The human-animal bond allows our pets to capture a part of our hearts we never knew existed. They come right in and give us the unconditional love many humans long for without asking for anything in return. Those who provide

---

34   Françoise Mathieu, "What Is Compassion Fatigue?" *Tend Academy*, 2019.

care to stray, rescue, and companion animals experience a level of compassion and empathy, without which caring for animals may have never come into existence. Veterinary wellbeing advocate Marie Holowaychuk discusses the effects of empathy fatigue in comparison to compassion fatigue.

In veterinary practice, there is no shortage of situations whereby an animal or pet owner is suffering and a veterinary caregiver experiences emotional empathy in response. When an owner is struggling with the decision to treat or euthanize their pet, saddened by the news of a terminal illness, or stricken by grief upon hearing that their pet is not responding to treatment, veterinary caregivers can identify, understand, and even *experience* the same feelings that the owner is experiencing. Unfortunately, this can lead to debilitating consequences if veterinary caregivers experience this repeatedly without taking time away from work to rest, refuel, and engage in self-care.[35]

Eventually, as a practice professional starts to realize the toll this takes, it becomes difficult to explain to friends, family, or a spouse. Coming home after a long day of work, mentally and physically exhausted, you want to rest. You want to lay on the couch or go to bed and process your day. Sometimes going home and having dinner doesn't happen. Normalcy becomes difficult to achieve, and the job begins to wear on you. "We're determined, passionate people who are used to putting our clients and our animals before ourselves. But these traits, which make us good doctors, are the same things

---

35 Marie Holowaychuk, "Is Empathy Good or Bad for Veterinary Caregivers?" *LinkedIn*, June 19, 2019.

that make us more susceptible to depression, anxiety and letting negative emotions chip away at us."[36]

Ashley, a licensed veterinary technician since 2009 shared with me,

> It's almost as if your tolerance and willingness to help or be stretched thin at work decreases. The desire and the passion begin diminishing, and you have to take a deep breath, go home and do those self-care things that restore you back to feeling like yourself again.

It takes a toll on people differently. In some it presents itself as anger, depression, and sadness, and it contributes to veterinary professionals being unhappy and leaving jobs. This in turn contributes to the lower pay rates, particularly for technicians because anyone can come in and learn the job and get paid half the salary of a licensed professional.

All of these components culminate in the perfect storm, leading to burnout, compassion fatigue, and the suicide epidemic plaguing the profession.

THE SUICIDE EPIDEMIC PLAGUING THE PROFESSION

We're often attacked by our clients for not responding to their requests on their time and referred to as lazy and not detail-oriented. The unbalanced demands of the job make it

---

36 David Leffler, "Suicides among Veterinarians Become a Growing Problem," *The Washington Post*, January 23, 2019.

difficult to juggle all of the responsibilities and requirements our employers, peers, and clients expect.

A particular event stuck in my memory comes to mind. We had a long-time client call our clinic about her dog Jack. Jack's rear legs gave out, he couldn't walk, and started vomiting. Jack required an extensive workup that our clinic couldn't provide him at the time. The appointment schedule and drop off schedule consisted of a full book of sick patients, within which we couldn't provide the level of care and workup Jack needed.

The receptionist gave Jack's owner the option to go to the emergency clinic. A couple hours later, I received an email about a negative review posted to our social media account as well as an email delineating the contempt this client felt about her interaction with the receptionist.

The media has become so prominent in allowing cyber-bullying, rating businesses, and creating content from only one perspective. At the end of the day, no time existed to see Jack and the staff already depleted all of their energy finishing out the day. In an effort to protect the team, the receptionist made a call she believed best for Jack and the mental health of her team.

On a similar note, the generous act of accommodating the special circumstances of a client with a sick pet can have detrimental effects on the whole team. Dr. Bowden, for example, pushed through a relentlessly challenging day, and just as the end was within sight—minutes away, in fact—a pet owner walked in with a sick cat. Anticipating a simple diagnosis like a UTI, Dr. Bowden agreed to see the patient. The cat, as it turned out, had a urinary obstruction, and if an obstruction prevents the bladder from emptying, the bladder could burst.

Dr. Bowden explained the risks and advised her client to take her cat to the emergency room. The pet's treatment needs went beyond what she and her staff could provide at closing time, she explained. The emergency clinic, fortunately, could provide excellent care after hours. The client said she couldn't afford to go to the emergency clinic. Angry that Dr. Bowden was unable to keep the clinic staff after hours to provide care, she lashed out at the doctor. "You're going to make me murder my pet because I can't afford to go to the emergency clinic? Why are you even a veterinarian? You clearly don't care about animals."[37]

Dr. Bowden reached her breaking point. On the verge of tears, she didn't want the client to see how deeply she impacted her, Dr. Bowden went back to her team and said, "These people really don't deserve our compassion. All of us are here because we care. So, I need three people to volunteer and stay late and help me treat this." Dr. Bowden performed the procedure to unblock the cat's bladder, and she did so at a discounted rate. In her TED talk, she said she did it because she couldn't endure another perceived "failure" in her already strenuous day. No good deed, as they say, goes unpunished, and Dr. Bowden's punishment would be waiting for her when she returned to work the next day. The hospital manager didn't support her decision

---

[37] *TED*, "Melanie Bowden: What Being a Veterinarian Really Takes," March 10, 2020, video, 19:04.

to conduct an after-hours procedure at a discounted rate. She deducted the equivalent of the discounted fees from the doctor's next paycheck.[38]

Veterinarians use many of the same types of equipment, medications, diagnostic testing, and expertise as human doctors. The up-front costs as clinicians and business owners are very comparable, but we charge drastically less. Why? Because otherwise most people wouldn't be able to afford medical care for their animals. As a profession, we take a pay cut to keep prices reasonable for the public.[39]

There are few circumstances more soul crushing in the career of a pet health professional than those involving a pet whose suffering you have the skills and ability to treat and a devoted pet owner who absolutely cannot afford the cost of treatment. This gut-wrenching experience can lead the thoughts of some veterinarians to a dark place. After a grueling day, they may sit and contemplate whether the pains of the profession are greater than the rewards.[40]

We do what we do because we are passionate about pet health and compassionate by nature. But sometimes, humans make it difficult to focus on the pet. For some, character accusations, threats, and negative remarks can chip away at any joy we experience as veterinary professionals. There's no escape, except to repeat this pattern of burnout for the next thirty years. Deeply in debt and deeply depressed, more and more

---

38 *TED*, "Melanie Bowden: What Being a Veterinarian Really Takes," March 10, 2020, video, 19:04.
39 Ibid.
40 Ibid.

veterinarians suffer silently until their desperate search for a way out compels them to take their lives.

It's tragic. And it's unacceptable to ignore it. Fortunately, brave voices and outspoken advocates have begun to bring to light the challenges faced by the veterinary industry. Change will come as those who can influence the profession unite to bring awareness to the topics of job burnout, compassion fatigue, and the suicide epidemic.

Professional organizations and corporations throughout the pet health industry are forming support groups, having open discussions, and training veterinary professionals to become advocates within the workplace. Together, we can improve the lives of the people who dedicate themselves to improving the lives of our pets. And you—as pet owners, high level management, and clients—have the ability to influence the outcome for the profession, too. If everyone exhibited a little bit more compassion and empathy, if more of us understood the realities of a day in the life of a veterinary professional, we might provide the additional support required to help make a veterinary career sustainable and to keep talented professionals in it for the long haul.

A HEALTHIER WORK-LIFE BALANCE

When Dr. Julie Potter, a practicing veterinarian of twenty-five years, started a family, she hoped her employer would provide the flexibility required by her special circumstances. Childcare options for a baby born with special needs were scarce. And without any family living nearby to provide support, Dr.

Potter would need additional time away from the practice to care for her newborn son. Her discussion with her employer hardly went as she'd anticipated. "We're sorry you're going through this," began her employer's response," but we no longer need you to work here."

Dr. Potter left the clinic devastated, hurt, and upset. The people for whom she had worked for so many years had neither offered to help her establish a schedule nor entertained the notion of creating a balance that allowed her to both care for her son and make a living. Employers' failure to accommodate such requests or understand the demands of normal life events sets people back in the profession. Female veterinary professionals make up the majority of the veterinary workforce, and the limited support after childbirth is alarming. For maternity leave, companies pay out the unused portion of vacation balances. Or the new mother can sign up for short-term disability and take the rest of the time off unpaid.

The expense of raising a child and seeking childcare services in this country have reached a new peak, making it not only difficult for a working mother to continue to work but also forcing her to choose between her profession and her family. The veterinary community can reach out and seek initiatives to support working parents. Whether companies create specific childcare options, increase pay so a mother can afford childcare services, or incorporate childcare options like some human hospitals do, this could alleviate some of the concern for working parents.

If we could provide our technicians, doctors, and support staff with reasonable wages, predictable scheduling, and necessary training and support, it would go a long way toward making our support staff happy. Dr. Coleman alluded to a need for flexibility in her work. "Providing flexibility to do the things that I want to do, that make me happy in my life, and use my PTO that I've earned would make me happier. But when there are a ton of limitations on that, then maybe I don't want to work for you."

At the end of the day, every day, veterinary professionals sacrifice their personal lives and well-being for the sake of their patients. When veterinarians graduate from vet school, they take an oath. The Veterinarian's Oath is:

> Being admitted to the profession of veterinary medicine, I solemnly swear to use my scientific knowledge and skills for the benefit of society through the protection of animal health and welfare, the prevention and relief of animal suffering, the conservation of animal resources, the promotion of public health, and the advancement of medical knowledge.
>
> I will practice my profession conscientiously, with dignity, and in keeping with the principles of veterinary medical ethics.
>
> I accept as a lifelong obligation the continual improvement of my professional knowledge and competence.[41]

If the veterinary community begins to understand the different job roles of each professional within a hospital, recognizes when a colleague is about to hit rock bottom, and works

---

41 AVMA. "Veterinarian's Oath," AVMA Policies, accessed May 21, 2020.

together to carry the job responsibilities, we can develop a proactive rather than a reactive approach to handling crises. Veterinarians sacrifice their:

- Financial security
- Credit
- Ability to travel or visit family
- Mental health
- Social life
- Wellbeing

They do their best in vet school and on the job to provide the best care for your pet and educate you as a client to make the best health decisions for your pet. The words from one of my colleagues were so powerful I believe everyone should hear them. This veterinarian stated,

> I knew what I signed up for when I chose this path, and even though it is rough I STILL want to do it because I am willing to sacrifice all of those things about my own life to save your animal. Your pet is that important to me. Your livestock operation is that important to me. The giraffe at the zoo is that important to me. So, the next time you think we are greedy, money hungry, or apathetic—remember me.

Pet ownership is a privilege, not a right. When people decide to adopt a pet, it's important to familiarize yourself with what to expect financially when owning a pet. By doing so, you have the power to prolong the life of your pet and understand that owning a pet comes with financial responsibilities to ensure their well-being.

In some cases, pet insurance can help combat some of the financial stress of pet ownership. Insurance plans usually have a monthly premium and an annual deductible that covers a wide range of services from preventative care to emergencies and allows pet owners and veterinary professionals to partner and care for the pets as a team.

Dr. Coleman shared some very insightful feedback on how to face some of the challenges surrounding the cost of pet care.

> It's a hard battle when you run into an emergency with a pet and you don't have insurance. You end up dipping into your savings and if you don't have that then you have to make a choice. It's heartbreaking for the staff to see, but the difficult reality is that you can't always help them all even if that's what you want to do. It's also hard not to say, when people you know should be responsible if they have pets. They should have a backup plan, but how many people in this country even have a reliable savings? And they might have rescued the dog or saved them from a bad situation. Or maybe they didn't mean to get it, and their child brought a pet home. Imagine being itchy around the clock but don't want to spend the money on the special food and the pills. It's hard to understand what that looks like when you're just looking at a little puppy who looks so cute and healthy. Letting a dog chew its feet off because it seems fine, is a miserable life for a pet to live. We can't control all these situations, but we should be able to help. We're not going to pay for the dog for its whole life, but if it has a one-time thing, and we educate the client on how to prepare for a financial

future with a pet then we can have an impact on the future life of that pet.

When practice professionals feel empowered to work on their strengths and develop their skills, they feel better about their jobs. If a senior employee could give a newer or less experienced employee the time of day and educate and train them on the different components of their jobs, they would feel much more confident, appreciated, valued, and whole. If the daily stressors came out into the open, maybe job burnout would decrease. If a series of difficult cases came in one week, talking about them or recognizing effects of those cases on the group of individuals could combat compassion fatigue. If the day-to-day stressful triggers became better controlled, maybe veterinarians wouldn't feel the need to resort to suicide or quit the profession to evade the problems. Lastly, if we prioritized a healthy work-life balance, an entirely different perspective and feel for the veterinary industry could form, and the profession could become attractive again.

CHAPTER 6

BRIDGE THE GAP

Several years ago, I worked with a veterinarian who was prone to misdirect her stress toward the staff. Instead of rationally evaluating situations, she would lose her cool and lash out at members of the team. She lacked the capacity to track the root causes of errors and shortfalls. One evening, Katie, a veterinary assistant in training, and I worked a busy closing shift with this particular veterinarian. Katie couldn't do much with triaging the appointments because of her limited experience so we did the best we could with caring for the incoming pet patients and the boarding pets. The situation could've been better, but we were determined to get through it.

I greeted the next client, weighed the patient, took a patient history, and briefed the veterinarian. She went into the exam room to converse with the client and develop a treatment plan. While the vet performed the exam, Katie and I took care of the boarders and checked in with the vet every five minutes to see if she needed assistance. Once her patient had been examined and her client was out of earshot, the vet came out of the room and approached Katie and me. She was visibly agitated. Then, right in front of our new employee, she yelled at me.

"You're not doing your job, Neha!"

At that moment, I realized the way she treated me and my colleagues was unacceptable. When individuals work hard and invest in their jobs, they deserve respect and understanding from those they work with.

This chapter is about the gap between members of staff, who don't always understand—or even try to understand—what it's like to be in each other's position. Now that we understand the different roles in the profession and what it takes to be a veterinary professional, we can analyze some techniques to help bridge the gaps that exist between veterinary professionals tasked to work in different roles on the same team. The stress level in the environment can contribute to causes, misperceptions, and misunderstandings among peers. If we collaborate to address the root causes of this friction, we can move the profession forward.

SEEK TO UNDERSTAND

The situation I've just described made me feel degraded, unappreciated, and angry. When the veterinarian yelled at me in front of Katie, she didn't realize by doing so she started shaping Katie's opinion of the workplace and her colleagues. If I were in Katie's shoes, I would run home! A job where the veterinarian thinks it is appropriate to demean her staff doesn't look the slightest bit appealing to me. My job consisted of numerous responsibilities. I tried to complete the list of tasks that included checking on the pets in the hospital needing care, completing housekeeping items, and ensuring all tasks on the daily checklist were marked complete. Despite completing these duties, the veterinarian responded by saying I wasn't doing my job.

Before placing blame and accusations on others, you should ask a series of questions before you react. Consider asking yourself the following:

- Does my colleague understand the various roles on the team and how they interconnect?
- Has my colleague received adequate training on required job responsibilities?
- Have we as a team agreed upon common goals and objectives for our clinic and identified nonnegotiable items and standards?
- Do I have the skills and knowledge to help my colleague perform their job better?
- Have I created an open environment where I can ask for and offer help?

When the veterinarian lashed out on me, I felt like she personally attacked me. As I evolved into a leadership role, I looked back on situations like this one to try to better understand where the disconnect happened. How much did she have on her plate and I on mine? In her training as a veterinarian, did she learn how to navigate difficult situations or practice soft skills? Maybe she didn't have an environment to openly discuss what caused her stress and work toward solutions.

Delving into the cause of how this particular situation arose, I quickly realized that our operating processes were broken. The redundancy in the steps and repeating the same task multiple times overworked the staff. Our process looked like this: the vet went into the room, examined the pet, discussed the plan with the client, and then came out to repeat the discussion that occurred in the exam room to the technician. This happened for every appointment, every day. It ate up time that could've been spent on other tasks. Many veterinary assistants and technicians appreciated not having to stay in the exam room the entire time with the vet, but the efficiency of appointments couldn't have been worse. Duplicating steps led to lost time and money and resulted in a limited number of staff working a busy shift because the payroll didn't allow for additional support.

On another note, different generations of veterinarians routinely practiced different styles of veterinary medicine. I spoke with an LVT, Ashley, who shared her frustrations at her former veterinary clinic. She described the disconnect between her and a veterinarian she used to work with. Ashley voiced that when working with different generations of veterinarians, assistants, and technicians the older, traditional methods of practicing medicine compared to upgraded methods didn't flow seamlessly. The newer generations of veterinary professionals came out of school with different resources and knowledge than their predecessors. This created an obvious gap when it came to treating pets or communicating treatment plans within the clinic.

Similar to Ashley's clinic, many clinics experienced confusion among the veterinary team and clients. The gap became increasingly more apparent when each veterinarian followed a different treatment protocol for a medical condition. To lessen the discrepancy in treatment options, veterinarians should work with their colleagues and establish a common set of practices. By establishing a baseline, the team and the clients could work together more effectively instead of questioning why one veterinarian treated a medical condition one way and another veterinarian another way.

Ashley shared insight about how times have changed and how veterinary teams can come together to find better ways of implementing new practices while utilizing years of experience tenured individuals bring to the table.

> The best way to set your pre-medication protocols or how to treat a skin infection have changed within veterinary medicine. I've personally experienced that we learn a certain way in tech school of how to do things which is based on the AVMA regulations that accredited that school. I feel like there's a fresh perspective and newer teachings new grads bring, but it isn't always favorable when you're in a practice with older practitioners. I think that there is more than one way to do something, and if it makes someone else uncomfortable because they learned a different way, I don't necessarily think just because it's your way to do it, it's the right way to do it. So, there's frustration there. I definitely feel like there's more leniency and understanding in that aspect from the younger generation of veterinarians. But like I said, each group of individuals has a unique perspective and skillset to teach and learn from because these methods aren't

always taught in school but gained through experience by working in a veterinary practice.

Having an open mind and learning from one another makes a world of difference when a graduate transitions from the academic clinical environment to a professional veterinary practice. Throughout the years of experience veterinary professionals have had, some learned how to restrain a pet patient in school or on the job. This didn't necessarily mean that one person over another possessed the knowledge to do so in the most effective way. If a clinic professional had always done something one way, it doesn't necessarily mean it's the best way either. Collaboration and open-mindedness help individuals advance in their roles and function more effectively within a veterinary practice.

CROSS-TRAINING AND LEVERAGING EMPLOYEES

Early on, I learned that each member plays a significant role in the overall functioning of a practice. To alleviate bottlenecks in a process, pay attention to everyone's strengths and weaknesses. In a veterinary setting, very few tasks can be done alone. From the time an appointment lands on the schedule to the time the pet enters the hospital, the process of providing care for that pet requires effective collaboration throughout the entire staff.

One common hurdle in a veterinary clinic affecting cross-functional teams resulted when a receptionist misinformed a client of what services their pet was due for. This adversely affected the ability of the team to care for the pet because of the discrepancy in expectations set at the time of the phone call. By cross-training employees, we can foster greater inter-department understanding, empower individuals to step in and provide support when needed, and encourage individuals to consider their colleagues' perspectives. I've always thought this when complaining and dissatisfaction heighten, sometimes you have to take a walk in someone else's shoes to truly understand the capacity of their job role.

In an article by Corey Bleich of EdgePoint Learning, he describes the importance of cross-training while being aware of the risk of burnout.

> Imagine the three legs of a stool. If one leg falls off, the stool is useless. Now imagine a company in which only one employee knows anything about a process or a procedure. What happens if that person takes maternity leave or becomes ill and needs time off? Cross-training employees holds up the seat of your business, even when your resident expert steps away. This makes your business more sustainable, even in times of transition.[42]

COMMUNICATION

In an article by the Society of Human Resource Management in 2013, four hundred corporate businesses with over one hundred thousand employees were surveyed and found

---

42 Cory Bleich, "6 Major Benefits to Cross-Training Employees," *EdgePoint, LLC (blog)*.

that communication barriers cost the average organization $62.4 million per year in lost productivity. Effective communication refers to communication between two or more people with the purpose of delivering, receiving, and understanding the message successfully. It's the process of information sharing between team members in a way that takes into account what you want to say, what you actually say, and what your audience interprets.[43] Whether you manage employees, supervise colleagues, coordinate a team of volunteers, interact with clients, or implement change management initiatives, your ability to communicate effectively with others directly effects leadership outcome.

Paige Arnof-Fenn, founder & CEO of Mavens & Moguls, suggests leaders use the right communication channels and keep them open at all times.

> Communication is key to our employee engagement and success, so I try to set the tone upfront with one rule, when in doubt over-communicate. Especially now that everyone is working remotely it is key to set up regular video and conference calls with your team. At the beginning of the project do not make assumptions about what people from different groups want or know, just ask or send an e-mail. It will save you a lot of time, money and frustration down the road. Trust me. This comes from experience. Be a good listener and make sure you hear the others, their hopes, frustrations, and intentions. If the lines of communication are open and everyone makes an effort to listen and be

---

43 "The Cost of Poor Communication," *SHRM*, 2013.

heard then collaboration will happen naturally, and the information will flow.[44]

I have found that communication workshops during staff meetings help decrease gaps within an organization. During these workshops, members of the team learn to better understand one another's communication styles, which leads to less miscommunication down the road. When I started out as a practice manager, we held numerous communication workshops. A particularly fun one identified communication styles based on dog breed. The employees identified strongly with this workshop as we all worked in a veterinary practice.

Conducting communication workshops helps cultivate a culture of effective communication. Tips on how to do so, as mentioned by Rachel Summers, a social media management professional, are:

- **Schedule meetings:** Meetings allow for everyone to meet and discuss current events in a business, challenges, and explore solutions. They allow everyone to communicate and collaborate with each other, as well as give everyone an opportunity to ask questions and ask for what they may need from one person to the next. Oftentimes busy schedules limit the amount of time people can spend asking questions or providing feedback.
- **Recognize the positive:** Communications don't always have to be negative. It is important to have positive conversations frequently with colleagues rather than only

---

44 Rachel Summers, "How to Communicate Effectively with Your Team," *ProSky*, March 31, 2020.

when they make a mistake, or something isn't working. It is important to recognize what is working well.
- **Use the correct channels to communicate that work for your team and clients:** There are so many different methods of communication these days; IM, email, text, phone, etc. It is important to formulate a plan for your team and clients to determine what the best way to communicate is. For example, when communicating with anyone, whether a colleague or a client, it is important to ask what the best method of contact is in order to ensure your message is sent and received by the person you are communicating with.
- **Set deadlines and expectations, and then check-in.**
- **Check your grammar, edit, and proofread:** This is important because it allows an effective message to be sent rather than words thrown out there that may not signify the message effectively.
- **Don't interrupt others:** It is easy to interrupt someone when they are speaking and not listen to what they have to say. When someone is talking, it is important to take a second and absorb what was said and then display understanding by repeating back to the individual a short summary of what they meant to make sure both parties are on the same page.
- **Write it down:** It is easy to forget what someone may say in a busy practice. Therefore, documenting the conversation or taking notes is a good way to remember the important points of the conversation. In a medical practice, especially with client communications, it is crucial to record what the client said. That way, there is record of what was said and requested vs. having to go off memory,

which isn't always reliable when having conversations with multiple people at the same time.
- **Stick to the facts**: Oftentimes messages can be misinterpreted, and people can bring opinions and personal thoughts into the scenario. Sticking to the facts will allow for more direct communication without outside influences which may be unprofessional.
- **Think before you speak**: Sometimes we can blurt out words which may not deliver the message that was intended.
- **Continue to share your company's values**: Sharing company and team values on a regular basis reminds individuals about why they are on the team and a client of the business.[45]

The more we communicate with each other, the likelihood of closing the gaps of miscommunication increases. Being direct, clear and specific, paying attention to nonverbal cues, listening, and staying positive and respectful aid in effective communication.

EMOTIONAL INTELLIGENCE

Another component of effective communication incorporates emotional intelligence. Without emotional intelligence, key communication skills remain undeveloped. Emotional intelligence encompasses at least three skills: the ability to identify and name one's own emotions, or "emotional awareness"; the

---

45 Rachel Summers, "How to Communicate Effectively with Your Team," *ProSky*, March 31, 2020.

ability to harness those emotions and apply them to tasks like thinking and problem-solving; the ability to manage or regulate one's emotions when necessary and to help others do the same.[46]

As veterinary professionals, we can bridge the gap by learning about and incorporating emotional intelligence in our communication with others. Sometimes when team members have outbursts, even *they* don't understand why they've reacted with such emotion. They may feel certain emotions but not know how to describe them. When we understand our own emotions as well as those of others, we can have more engaging and forgiving conversations. We give ourselves and each other space to work through emotions without fear of being viewed as "too emotional."

That's not to say an outburst of emotions is always acceptable or appropriate, but more intelligent conversations can take place to discover the root of a problem. Emotional intelligence and the power of perspective can transform some of the relationships and judgments people often have. Adopting the mindset that everyone shares a different perspective and trying to come to a common ground can work wonders when it comes to working within a team. A colleague may have a better solution or analysis of the situation on hand than I do and can help unveil a new perspective. This allows us to grow as individuals and develop more effective communication habits if we can see things from someone else's eyes.

---

46 "Emotional Intelligence." *Psychology Today*, 2020.

THE BIG PICTURE

We spoke a lot about effective communication strategies. In the end, the bigger picture revolves around satisfying the needs of veterinary professionals and clients. As a larger community, we can partner together with the understanding that we want to share compassion in our interaction toward one another, help ease stress, and harbor positive workplace relationships.

When everyone involved understands the implications of how they communicate, their actions, and their reactions we create a team more inclusive and encompassing, rather than unhappy and distant. As veterinary professionals, we not only have to understand the importance of the roles and responsibilities of our own jobs, but also those of others we work with. Veterinarians should have a sound understanding of how the business operates and what the day-to-day of the support team looks like. Veterinary technicians and assistants should understand the day-to-day life of a veterinarian and a receptionist and vice versa. Clients should understand the major stressors and triggers for veterinary professionals, harbor more inclusive and productive relationships with veterinary professionals, and share their concerns in a professional manner.

No one's a punching bag or responsible for all of the hostility and grief that others feel. If we partner together, as a larger community of veterinary professionals and pet parents, I believe we can alleviate the gravity of compassion fatigue, depression, suicidal thoughts, and enhance job satisfaction within the profession. If everyone takes a step back to really understand another's perspective, I firmly believe more positive and inclusive workplaces will form, and we can guide the future of the profession.

PART 3

ADAPTING TO CHANGE

CHAPTER 7

CREATING A POSITIVE MINDSET

My friend Elizabeth has the rare ability to recognize where sadness lies. She could brighten your day, no matter who you are. She just—*knows*. Elizabeth Troncoso—we like to call her E.—has been a veterinary care professional since 1999 and a breast cancer survivor since 2015. Neither her career in the industry nor her battle with cancer has dulled her spirit. She's one of those people who wakes up every morning genuinely grateful to see yet another day. Elizabeth has faced her challenges head on by maintaining a positive mindset, and she applies that same mindset as she consoles her peers and clients with compassion and empathy.

When I met E., she worked as a client service representative (CSR) at a veterinary clinic. We worked together there, and to be honest, the role suited her so well that I sometimes forget she'd had another life before she came to work in a veterinary hospital. For years, Elizabeth worked as an accountant at a law firm. One day, something in her heart told her she no longer belonged at the law firm. And that was that. She quit. She didn't have a plan for her future. She just—*knew.* And sure enough, not long after she walked out on her old life, Elizabeth took her dog for a checkup and heard one of the staff members mention a need for administrative help. She applied for the role, joined the practice, and worked as a CSR for two years. *I love it when good things happen for good people.* Over time, she evolved into the role of practice manager. She didn't have a lick of knowledge on how to run a business, but she had the passion to learn.

"I knew I wanted to help people," she says, *"and I followed my heart."*

At the veterinary hospital, Elizabeth shifted the energy and formed partnerships with her clients. She'd tell them, "We'll worry about the money later, we'll work it out. Let's take care of what you need to take care of. You can't choose paying your rent and getting groceries or keeping your loved one alive. I think that's a very unfair choice."

That's when something unexpected began to happen.

"Once my clients saw that I made the choice to believe in them," Elizabeth says, "they believed in us and would show up with a gift basket of baked goods throughout the year to say thank you. It was like the light came into the hospital, and everything was good, because we did everything from our hearts."

Elizabeth worked day-in, day-out with her team and clients to celebrate successes of not only the business, but also the relationships they developed. Her heart thrived on building relationships and creating that warm, family-oriented environment for her team, clients, and the pets. After a few years in practice management, E. left that role and returned to her former position. She belonged there. In her heart, she just *knew*. Back in her old desk, my dear friend found ways to spread joy and gratitude beyond the walls of our veterinary hospital. Working alongside Dr. Jackson, Elizabeth helped create the clinic's "client card ministry." When clients made mention of major life events—whether joyful or sorrowful—he would make note to send them personalized cards. Elizabeth championed his kindness practice, continuing his legacy and commitment to demonstrating to clients that our team not only cared *for* pets but also cared *about* pet parents.

RELATIONSHIPS

Kindness has a tendency to spread. As the client card ministry's kindness touched more and more clients, relationships developed. Referrals increased. New clients became loyal clients and sources of referrals too. Generations and extensions of client and employee families came into our clinic with their pets, and our network grew.

According to an article in the *Journal of Retailing and Consumer Services,* a study examined how customer gratitude determined the success or failure of a firm's relationship marketing.

> The study confirmed the role of *customer gratitude* between the customers' perceptions, a firm's

relationship marketing investments and customers' perceptions of the *value of the relationship* with the firm. For theorists, this customer gratitude model offers a better psychological explanation of how relationship marketing investments operate to improve the value that customers place on their relationships with retailers. Our research suggests that managers should invest resources to stimulate customer gratitude in order to build strong customer–seller relationships.[47]

"It makes a difference in any business when you have people that want to come by and say hello when they don't have business with you that day," Elizabeth says.

Soon the veterinary team became a part of the pets' family. Our colleagues and clients built friendships inside and outside our workplace. And it all began with small gestures.

Elizabeth hoped our relationships with our clients could ignite camaraderie within teams and allow colleagues to form sustainable relationships with one another. It worked. Inspired by our clients' positivity, we became a more grateful, thoughtful team. We said "please" and "thank you" to each other, a seemingly small—and necessary—gesture that can contribute to a more engaged staff. And an engaged staff is a happier staff.

In the Grant and Gino study, psychologists Adam Grant and Francesca Gino studied the effects of gratitude. They found that:

---

47 Syed Fazal E. Hasan, et al., "The Role of Customer Gratitude in Making Relationship Marketing Investments Successful," *Journal of Retailing and Consumer Services* 21, no. 5 (September 2014):788.

Gratitude is a non-monetary way to support those non-monetary motivations. "Thank you" doesn't cost a dime, and it has measurably beneficial effects. In a series of four experiments, they found that "thank you" from a supervisor gave people a strong sense of both self-worth and self-efficacy. The study also reveals that the expression of gratitude has a spillover effect: Individuals become more trusting with each other, and more likely to help each other out.[48]

HARBORING A POSITIVE WORKPLACE CULTURE

My veterinary family understands the stressors of the workplace, and we can get together at any time and talk through our problems, grievances, discuss solutions, and be there for each other when those outside the field may not understand everything that goes into it.

Creating a positive workplace culture directly impacts workplace relationships—the relationships you build at work, relationships at home, and relationships with clients and pets. You're probably wondering how veterinary professionals have time to build relationships when they rarely have enough time to take a lunch break. In a veterinary practice, veterinary professionals work so closely together that the effects of a toxic work environment infect everybody quickly. To avoid such from happening, healthy workplace relationships are necessary because at any time

---

48 Jeremy A. Smith, "Five Ways to Cultivate Gratitude at Work," *The Greater Good Science Center at the University of California, Berkeley*, May 16, 2013.

you may need to call on one of your teammates to assist with a patient or swap in for a last-minute shift. If these relationships don't exist, the ability to collaborate and have positive work experiences diminishes.

When you work with someone forty or more hours per week, working relationships naturally develop. The hard work comes into play when it comes time to maintain them. Having staff meetings, team outings, conversations about life goals, and learning about each other makes for an encompassing partnership rather than a formal relationship that ends once you're off the clock.

In my experience, I have seen many employees who started off solely as coworkers and became the best of friends. As they developed a relationship of mentor and mentee and got to know one another, the relationship changed. It became so strong that they swiftly accomplished any and all tasks that came their way. They continued to mentor, coach, and guide their peers as forthcoming industry professionals.

From my friend Elizabeth, I learned to accept that each day presented with a different set of challenges, and how I handled them was up to me. Any day walking into the clinic could start off with two employees' not getting along because one came in late or because a machine broke down in the midst of a procedure. As a hospital manager, my team always looked to me to resolve the differences and problems. Now you see, fairness in these situations didn't always exist, but it came with the territory. As a leader, I had to ensure I set the tone for the clinic.

Throughout my experiences, I learned the importance of creating a workplace culture that harbored growth, collaboration, and positivity. This led to creating a list of nonnegotiable items as a team. We decided to hold each other accountable for the following items every day, no matter what:

1. Remember to respect and appreciate each other.
2. If you can't smile, go home and find it.
3. No complaining without a solution.

This type of culture fostered a growth mentality and collaborative workplace relationships. Team members worked together to meet a common goal, provide quality patient care, and excellent customer service. At the same time, it amazed me to see how they picked each other up when one struggled to get through the day. If a disagreement or concern arose between management and staff, an open environment existed where both parties could discuss their concerns and work toward solutions together.

Elizabeth taught me that I can choose my attitude every day. When I choose to be grateful that I have a job and remind myself that I'm making a difference in a pet's life, my heart fills with warm fuzzies. I don't think I can go wrong with that attitude. A veterinary practice has no room for negativity. We must choose to be positive for the sake and health of the animals and each other.

HOW TO PRACTICE BEING GRATEFUL

Elizabeth claims to have inherited a deep sense of gratitude from her father. Both father and daughter, she says, innately felt it a duty to share their gratitude and positive outlook with others. For most of us, however, gratitude requires practice. Learning how to feel and express gratitude takes time but leads to more of a fulfilling sense of self in the long run. Two good starting points, reflection and thankfulness, allow the feelings of gratitude to persevere. Elizabeth shared a wonderful life lesson with me, "When you feel gratitude, you can't feel negativity. It's impossible. So that's one of the biggest secrets, being grateful for even waking up in the morning and carrying that attitude with you throughout the day."

I can tell you, before I shifted my mindset from being bogged down by all of the challenges I would have to face walking into the clinic, I dreaded waking up or going in. Sometimes I thought about calling in sick. But my will was stronger than the intimidation of the daily challenges I faced. I had accepted this leadership role. Accepting and understanding my role as a leader, I had to coach my team. I worked with them through solving complex problems and adopting a different mindset.

Because pets are unpredictable, even scheduled procedures can exceed the time allotted for them. This is especially true of dental procedures. A typical dental visit might include dental x-rays and a professional dental cleaning, performed under anesthesia. Dental x-rays detect diseased or infected teeth, which usually necessitates a tooth extraction. When the need for dental surgery to extract teeth arises, there may very well be two or three more procedures still in queue. In my experience, that often meant the team couldn't break for lunch. I would order pizzas or sub-in for them so they could take thirty minutes to step away and recharge. Admittedly, this still wasn't the ideal situation, but they generally appreciated my gesture. We worked together, we made it work.

Another way I expressed gratitude for my team as they worked through a busy procedure day was by completing charges while the surgery techs continued to prep for the next surgery, monitor anesthesia, and assist the doctor with the procedure or I would offer to sub-in as the surgery tech so they could complete the tasks mentioned above. Many times, our surgery technicians worked through the afternoon, and completing the billing, discharge instructions, and filling the medications took a chunk of time off their already hectic and strenuous day. In turn, this kept the team functioning at high efficiency and allowed the clinic to provide complete care to the patients.

Recognizing the contribution someone makes, how it impacts the bigger picture, and expressing gratitude can move mountains when it comes to having a positive attitude, navigating negativity, building relationships, and practicing how to be grateful. To start practicing how to be grateful, a few tips and tricks have helped me navigate through difficult situations and begin my day with an open heart. These tricks only take a few moments of your day but can make it flow so much better:

1. **Intention:** I would wake up every morning, think about the type of day that I wanted to have and plan for that

experience. Every day I'd say good morning to those I met or make an effort to say hello with a smile when I saw them. This set my day off to a positive start, and I shared the positive energy with those around me. They say people feed off of each other, so why not give each other positive energy to feed off of?

2. **Time:** I'd set aside quiet time to reflect. We live in a fast-paced world and barely have time to catch up with ourselves and absorb the day. From the moment we wake up to the moment we go to bed, we generally move at lightning speed and don't slow down. By scheduling quiet time every day to reflect, we give ourselves the chance to slow down and process all the good, bad, and the ugly from the day.

3. **Thought:** By taking time to reflect, we can also use this time to give thought to everything we do have. It is easier to think about everything we do not have, and why we don't have it. But there are so many things we do have that don't have to be material. How often do we reflect on everything we do have? I challenge you to take time each day and think about one to two things you do have that you may take for granted. Then give thanks for them.

4. **Generosity:** Be generous to those with less and not envious of those with more. We tend to look at what we lack in life, rather than what we have and compare ourselves to others. This type of thinking creates envy and jealousy as opposed to satisfaction. What can we do to break that cycle? Volunteer at a local food bank or animal shelter on a regular basis, which reminds you how fortunate your situation is rather than focusing on what you do not have.

5. **Acknowledge:** Lastly, tell those you love how thankful you are for having them in your life. So many times, we neglect to take the time to craft the words to express appreciation for those closest to us and what their presence in our lives means to us. Take the opportunity to write them a note, make a phone call, or send a message. Let them know what they mean to you, and in return you'll begin to create the possibility of deeper connected and more fulfilling relationships with those you love.

These five tips are just a starting point of how to practice gratefulness. Many different ways to do this exist and can really change your perspective about a difficult part of the job, for example client education. Client education is a very taxing, time-consuming, and rigorous exercise in many industries. By changing my outlook on how I repeatedly had to recite the same information multiple times per day, I changed my outlook and became grateful to have the tools to educate pet owners and recommend services to help diagnose disease early in pets.

Creating positive, fulfilling experiences in a workplace requires consistency and accountability for one's actions and job responsibilities. When things start to slip and there's a lack of accountability, a negative and toxic workplace starts forming. People seek out problems rather than solutions, they breakdown the weak, ostracize those who don't engage in the drama, and shift the culture in the wrong direction. I want to surround myself with positive, enthusiastic people who appreciate and feel excitement about the opportunity they have today, one that many people don't have.

CHAPTER 8

TOOLS FOR VETERINARY PROFESSIONALS

———

How many times have you entered a profession fully equipped to balance your work life and personal life?

We develop and refine our personal financial skills, interpersonal skills, and personal wellness habits as we grow. The excitement of receiving that first paycheck may justify a small self-indulgence—maybe even a fancy, celebratory dinner. But as you embark on a career, you learn quickly that when the cash flow goes toward entertainment expenses, you can get caught up in a tug-of-war between paying bills or hanging out with friends. Young professionals—whatever your profession—may have to confront difficult decisions about where and how to spend this hard-earned money. Should I put my group outings on a credit card and pay the minimum balance later? *Speaking with many individuals and learning about how much they paid toward credit card interest rates surprised me!*

Along with personal financial habits, veterinary professionals discover they're ill-prepared to communicate with their colleagues and clients. They report that they had underdeveloped soft skills. Dr. Van Sickle, a practicing veterinarian of over twenty-five years, shares her experience and overall outlook on how she didn't feel equipped with the tools necessary to succeed as a veterinarian. She said, "When in vet school, I received no training on human psychology or how to communicate with people and had no warning about what to expect in the real world. I hope things have improved for new graduates, but I suspect there's still a lack of instruction in this area."

Veterinary professionals like her have an established career and clientele but say they still feel unhappy. Others say they love what they do and have found a reasonable balance, but struggle to move on in the wake of difficult situations with a client, pet, or colleague. Still others say they feel like they finally have figured it out. They love what they do and have found solutions to make their daily lives as a veterinary professional more meaningful, stress-free, and enjoyable.

When ill-equipped with the skills and tools required for a sustainable career, the stress and anxiety associated with the job can slowly chip away at the joy veterinarians and their teams may feel or have felt at work. In this chapter, we'll begin a discussion about the tools that can help veterinary professionals succeed and find balance in the profession. My heart breaks every time I hear that yet another veterinarian, technician, or practice professional has exited the field or lost the desire to continue practicing. Solutions do exist. We can help the veterinary community reignite a love for the field.

MENTORSHIP AND BUILDING A NETWORK

A balanced blend of highly experienced and less experienced practice professionals creates an ideal environment for mentorship. According to an article by the AVMA,

> Mentoring is defined as a relationship between an inexperienced person (protégé or mentee) and an experienced person (mentor) that will help the protégé learn from the mentor. New hire mentoring has the potential to help you navigate through an organization's procedures and politics and helps ease your transition into a new job. The more comfortable you are, the more likely you will feel a part of the team and remain employed at that job for a long time.[49]

Mentorship sets the bar high, becoming increasingly more common and more desired by veterinary professionals. Veterinary hospitals and companies should shift their focus to building a culture of training and development within their organizations. For example, if someone does dental cleanings very well, he or she should take an assistant or technician under their wing and teach them how to conduct the procedure. This type of collaboration allows for more consistent trainer/trainee feedback and learning to happen versus the traditional mindset of expecting individuals to learn on their own. Confident and well-rounded individuals integrate well with a practice when they have guidance and support.

---

49 AVMA, "New Hire Mentoring Programs," Career Articles, accessed September 15, 2020.

Similarly, Dr. Potter shared her experience in veterinary clinics where veterinarians hadn't developed inclusive working relationships. Dr. Potter worked as a relief veterinarian for multiple practices and had exposure to different personalities. She witnessed fear, competition, and jealously between vets. She saw vets fear another vet would steal a client or compete for commission in unprofessional ways. As a result, a toxic work environment and poor associate relationships formed.

Veterinarians could influence the future of the profession in a positive way by adopting a mentee. Taking part in associate mentorship creates inclusive working relationships, trust, and gives more freedom to those in senior level roles. By mentoring associates, you will find yourself with more freedom to go on a vacation, learn new skills, and grow into different positions. Leveraging the team makes this possible because the team can do more and share responsibilities instead of one or two expert vet professionals knowing how to do it all. Veterinary professionals can focus on creating collaborative teams and cohesive working relationships instead of perceiving one another as a threat.

Mentorship provides individuals an opportunity to build their leadership skills and allows mentees to feel more secure knowing that they have the support of a colleague to help them every step of the way. I can say I have seen numerous professional relationships develop into friendships full of camaraderie and happiness. These individuals feel more satisfied with their work and experience the freedom to take time off as needed versus feeling like they can never take time off because no one can do their job.

In an article released by the American Animal Hospital Association (AAHA), "Mentoring is a method to improve hospital culture, productivity, and efficiency. It has been shown to improve communication, promote long-term job satisfaction, and facilitate adoption of best practices. Ultimately, mentoring relationships can lead to improved patient care and overall hospital performance."[50] If pairing a new employee with an experienced one isn't part of your practice culture, it should be! Old and new generations of veterinary professionals desire mentorship.

SOFT SKILLS

Just like mentorship takes practice, the development of soft skills does too. Soft skills don't always come naturally and require practice. According to an article on Indeed.com, soft skills are any skill or quality that can be classified as a personality trait or habit. Employers search for candidates who possess interpersonal skills and communication skills. In a recent survey of one thousand hiring managers, we asked them to list the most important attributes of top performers at their company. The top five attributes they named were:

- Problem-solving
- Effective communication skills
- Self-direction
- Drive
- Adaptability/Flexibility[51]

---

50 John T. Tait, et al., "American Animal Hospital Association: Mentoring Guidelines," *Trends Magazine*, May/June 2008.
51 "Soft Skills: Definitions and Examples," Indeed Career Center, accessed September 15, 2020.

Soft skills come with on-the-job training, working on a team, interacting with clients, and through experiences that can help sharpen them. Valuable resources to aid with soft skill development exist in the forms of online courses, requesting feedback from others, working with a coach or mentor, and practice.[52] Soft skills in a veterinary practice ensure fluid communication between clients and staff and assist in navigating crises. Success in the profession combines mentorship and using soft skills to establish trusting relationships.

SETTING GOOD PERSONAL FINANCIAL HABITS

Another area in which veterinary professionals experience unsound stress revolves around finances. People don't readily have access to or have the knowledge around how to build good personal financial habits. This can alleviate stress for veterinary professionals.

In an interview, Dr. Lance Roasa, founder of drip.vet, explained that he and his team have developed methods to help new graduates develop healthy personal financial habits. The project was deeply personal for him. Dr. Roasa had lost a colleague to the veterinary suicide epidemic. Inspired to join forces to try to curb the tragic epidemic, Dr. Roasa and his colleague developed drip.vet. Drip.vet serves as an educational platform of online classes to help equip veterinarians with the personal success tools they need and aren't taught in veterinary school. Drip teaching methodology

---

52 "How to Identify and Develop Soft Skills," Glassdoor, accessed September 15, 2020.

teaches concepts in smaller quantities over time, referred to as drips. Smaller bits of information allow students to process, retain, and better understand course material in daily, digestible drips.

Currently, they have sixteen thousand veterinarians in the personal finance course. After six months of course work, students meet for a two-week retreat in Omaha, Nebraska. The course focuses on teaching veterinarians good habits and changing human behavior. The good habits consist of:

- Analyzing personal finance habits
- Teaching good spending habits
- Investing in a secure financial future
- Navigating away from living paycheck to paycheck

In addition to developing the Drip Teaching Method, Dr. Roasa and his colleague, Dr. Olsen, began reading and providing comments on multiple economic articles released by the American Veterinary Medical Association (AVMA). They chose to do this because the accuracy of the information isn't always 100 percent, due to no fault of the AVMA. Resources to statistically analyze the economics of the veterinary industry remain scarce other than the availability of surveys and assumptions. Surveying veterinarians upon graduation, technicians, businesses, and more serve as the primary methods to generate statistically significant numbers.

Veterinarians can benefit from programs like these. However, there should also be programs for other industry professionals who experience some of the same challenges when it comes to establishing good personal financial habits. An educational podcast, *Snack on This* by Edible Finance, follows a similar model in delivering bite-sized information for listeners to digest. In this podcast, bite-sized financial information educates listeners on how to plan for their future by learning about the basics of investing.

Veterinary schools currently do not teach personal financial skills, nor do veterinary technician programs. Both groups of individuals experience a two-to-one debt ratio and exhibit poor financial literacy. From personal experience, most individuals are fortunate if they learn personal finance habits from family members, personal research, or through financial coaches offered through banks. Otherwise, it's up to them to figure out how to create structured personal financial habits and goals on their own. Dr. Roasa left a piece of advice for future veterinary professionals.

> The world isn't stacked against you, but veterinarians have the ability and intelligence to make sound decisions about their financial future. By teaching personal finance, we can help veterinarians manage their finances and lower the debt to income ration. The debt to income ratio contributes to the veterinarian suicide epidemic as a major cause of stress.

FINANCIAL AID FOR CLIENTS

The fourth tool veterinary professionals and practices should consider, if they haven't already, is the option for an emergency pet fund and wellness plan in hospital. Donation funds allow for pet owners who do not have the means to pay for the treatment of their pet. Depending on the conditions for use of the funds, pet owners can qualify, and the hospital can use these funds to care for that pet.

Dr. Coleman worked as the lead veterinarian at a veterinary practice that provided financial aid for a pet in need. The purpose of the program was to defer shelter intake and treat curable conditions. Her practice raised money for a "Pet Retention Fund," which allowed them to provide discounted rates or grant money for pets who were in need of medical care and for owners who couldn't afford treatment.

> The general guidelines for someone to use pet retention was that it must be a curable condition. So, if your dog has chronic ear infections, we don't go down that road. But if your dog has a medical condition that is curable such as a pyometra, foreign body, or a broken leg we can ask to use funding from the pet retention fund. Some of these curable conditions tend to cost more and a lot of people might euthanize or watch their pet suffer through with or without a tragic end. It feels really good to have the ability to offer this type of assistance when pets need it.
>
> —DR. DESTINY COLEMAN

Veterinary practices could look to invest in emergency funds for patients in dire need of services when the owner may not be able to afford treatment. They could set them up similar to that of Dr. Coleman's clinic.

On the other hand, wellness plan packages provide options for pet owners regarding the expenses of their pets' care. Wellness plan packages typically divide up the cost into monthly payments and include all wellness services a pet would need for the year. If a client decides to move one day, having the option of transferring the plan with the pet allows for seamless and uninterrupted care. Larger organizations should consider optimizing patient record transfer, which also assures a client that the new location has the equipment and supplies necessary to provide care for their pet. Most wellness plan options offer a basic plan that includes preventative vaccinations and early disease detection testing (bloodwork, urinalysis, blood pressure, full body x-rays). They also have an elite package option that, oftentimes, includes a professional dental cleaning and dental x-rays.

By providing a wellness plan option, pet owners can budget for the cost of care, and on the flip side, veterinary professionals experience ease in charging for services and communicating with clients about routine procedures. Offering payment plan options such as wellness plans, educating pet owners about pet insurance, and offering Care Credit, a line of credit clients can apply for with 0% interest for a certain period of time, can help reduce stress and decisions that have to be made because of the cost of service. Doing so will allow veterinary professionals to practice better medicine and give clients the peace of mind that they can afford care for their pet.

Fun fact: the 25 percent of pet owners with pet insurance are 75 percent more likely to bring in their pet for immediate emergency care. We need to educate our clients about pet insurance and wellness plan options to give them security in affording the care of their pet, especially in a time of crisis.

VULNERABILITY AND PERSONAL WELLNESS

Lastly, veterinary professionals shouldn't shy away from being vulnerable. Veterinary professionals work long hours on their feet, experience difficult pets, clients, and cases. Expressing vulnerability and sharing how you feel with colleagues opens up the doors for deeper conversation and connection. According to Betsey Charles, DVM one of the biggest myths in veterinary medicine is that vulnerability signals weakness. We don't like asking for help. We fear that we'll look like we're not enough. Contrary to popular belief, you need to get comfortable being uncomfortable. Feeling the feels makes us uncomfortable. But when we do, that's what will help our profession thrive.[53]

Vulnerability goes hand in hand with focusing on self-care. We need to express ourselves in a healthy way and release the grief, stress, and emotion we feel after work. Oftentimes veterinary professionals don't have time to process numerous accounts of bad news delivered to a pet owner, or the number of euthanasia performed in a week. These cases are tough and break veterinary professionals down. Establishing self-care habits will help veterinary professionals feel better from the inside out.

---

53 Erica Tricarico, "Why Vulnerability Is Vital in Veterinary Medicine," *DVM360*, August 30, 2020.

Veterinary practices should implement self-care guidelines and create practice cultures focused on employee well-being. Resources exist to help create positive practice cultures and eliminate harmful habits that may have cultivated over the years.

Dr. Tannetje Crocker, a veterinarian practicing in Texas, shared with me how she's established healthy boundaries, developed a work-life balance that works for her, and earned a salary that fulfills the needs in her life. She accepted that not every practice suits her, she can't treat every pet, and she needs certain things in her life that make her happy and has created her life around that. When interviewing with potential employers, Dr. Crocker clearly laid out her expectations, salary, and schedule requirements and had them documented in her employment agreement. By taking ownership of her life and her job, she created a positive experience for herself and practiced high-quality medicine with respectful colleagues and built relationships with clients who valued what she had to offer.

In addition to vulnerability and personal wellness, the veterinary industry should start assessing the challenges that the aging veterinary workforce will face in the upcoming years. Working in a veterinary practice doesn't only affect us mentally, but it's also a physically taxing career. Implementing practice cultures around the physical wellness of employees will help retain the aging workforce. Every practice should consider substitute ways for lifting and handling large and small animals. A rolling stretcher or a lift table will aid personnel in lifting and moving heavy pets.

Considering the design of the hospital and developing a layout to support the aging workforce will prevent them from sustaining bodily injuries that could've been prevented. By focusing on the physical wellness of employees, veterinary organizations can develop ways to prevent the younger workforce from experiencing physical injuries or restrictions due to the physical requirements of the job.

Veterinary professionals experience a great amount of stress and responsibility on a daily basis, and the tools mentioned in this chapter as well as those in the upcoming chapters can help alleviate some of the grief and negativity around veterinary medicine. I hope that practice professionals and veterinary organizations continue to talk about the challenges facing the industry, and work toward solutions to improve them.

CHAPTER 9

ORGANIZING PROCESSES

"Crystal, have you seen Binkley's chart lying around? I can't find it."

Crystal has the superhuman abilities you want in your practice's customer service representative (CSR). She can juggle client relationships. She can always figure out how to make things right. And when you're frustrated, you can count on Crystal to cheer you up. It's widely rumored that our superhero CSR also has a "Spidey sense" for lost charts. When Crystal's on the hunt for a misplaced chart, it's almost as though she can *hear* missing charts calling out to her. On this particular day in 2014, I hoped Binkley-the-cat's chart would make itself known.

"He was just in for vaccinations this morning. Wasn't he?" she said, before giving me the universal sign for *Wait just a moment. I'm on the phone.* I continued my search until Crystal rushed me to the exam room for my next appointment,

"Go! Go! I have a couple of clients waiting for prescriptions, but I'll look for the chart as soon as I take care of them."

I'm embarrassed to admit how frequently team members misplace pet patient charts. I'm even more embarrassed to admit how much time and productivity the practice loses every time it happens. Sometimes for mere minutes, sometimes for hours, and occasionally a pet's chart would go missing for days.

This time, a few hours passed, but our heroic CSR emerged, Binkley's chart in hand. "Look what I found hanging out in the storage room."

There has to be a better way, I thought to myself.

There was. And a few months later, I led the practice through the process of learning and implementing that better way.

CONVERSION TO AN ELECTRONIC MEDICAL RECORD SYSTEM

In 2014, my team and I began preparations for our clinic's conversion to proprietary electronic medical record (EMR) software that had never been used in any other veterinary clinic.

Preparing to transition from paper medical records to electronic ones required meticulous preparation, training, and implementation. For four months, we studied, we trained, and we practiced. We took an online course. We learned to create invoices, enter medical notes and treatment plans, and then we used the training server to practice creating them ourselves.

If you've ever transitioned from a paper-based system to an electronic system of some kind, you'll understand what I mean when I say our existing workflow processes suddenly went from outdated to obsolete. We needed to build new processes. And that meant we could build them back better.

I analyzed our existing processes and eliminated redundancy. In our old system, we used the electronic medical record function in a limited capacity. Half of the record was electronic, and the other half was handwritten. To find notes on a medical condition, we looked through a paper record as well as the electronic one to paint a complete picture. The manual process of pulling paper records, filing papers, and documenting by hand took much more time compared to entering everything in an electronic record.

We could preset medical note templates and discharge instructions in a repository that allowed the veterinary team to copy and paste frequently used templates opposed to having to retype frequently used ones. This function streamlined part of the medical record entry process. The new software also allowed the veterinary team to email, fax, scan, and transfer records with just a few clicks. The conversion to an electronic medical record system thrilled me. Manual labor processes became automated and cut down on the amount of time wasted on redundant processes.

WASTE IN HEALTHCARE SYSTEMS

While leading the EMR conversion in 2015, I was also pursuing my MBA. It made for long days but also presented a silver lining. My Operations Management instructor invited a guest speaker from the Process Improvement department of INOVA Health Systems. He led us through a simulation of how a human hospital operates. The timing couldn't have been more ideal. We spent an hour in class learning about process improvement, and how excess time could be eliminated. The guest speaker split us into three groups to see the flow of the patient journey through the hospital. The components of the patient visit consisted of:

- The patient visiting the doctor
- The doctor ordering tests
- The front office staff working on billing and insurance
- The doctor communicating to the nurse patient care needed
- The doctor revisiting with the patient at the end of the appointment

During the simulation, one group of students focused on the patient flow, another the physician flow, and the third group kept track of the movement of the physician and the patient throughout the hospital.

Upon completion, my group determined two key factors directly made up the waste in the system: 1) the layout of the facility, and 2) the number of times the physician and patient walked back and forth. This class gave me a new perspective toward our processes at the clinic. I could see faulty processes and a flawed system and set out to learn how to improve them. I enrolled in Villanova University's Lean Six Sigma certification program in 2016 to pursue process improvement initiatives within my practice.

Systems and processes in human and veterinary health care vary widely. Some providers create their own systems, while others—in reality—make up the rules as they go. According to an article in the *Harvard Business Review,*

> It only takes 10 minutes of direct observation of a nurse in a hospital to understand care-delivery processes are not standardized and dependent on individuals, not systems. This lack of reproduction leads to errors. Since every caregiver does it his or her own way, it's difficult to improve anything. Stable systems that are reproducible are required to deliver consistently high quality. A process must first be stabilized then standardized before being improved. Because few standardized processes exist in care delivery many possibilities for error exist.[54]

In my Lean Six Sigma course at Villanova University, I learned about the eight common types of waste found in a healthcare system, referred to by the acronym DOWNTIME. DOWNTIME stands for the following:

- Defects
    - A computer system that doesn't save medical records

---

54 John S. Toussaint and Kathryn Correia, "Why Process Is US Healthcare's Biggest Problem," *Harvard Business Review,* March 19, 2018.

- An x-ray machine that stops working after taking an x-ray
- A pen that has ink but does not write

- Overproduction
    - Production of an item or service exceeds the demand
    - An excess number of cards are printed than will be used
    - Reply all on an email

- Waiting
    - Patient check-in delays due to not enough staff
    - Lag between doctor and technician duties
    - Client wait time when patients receive treatment

- Non-utilized Talent
    - Inflated job requirements that specify an advanced degree when the job can be done without it
    - Redundant training for experienced employees
    - Skilled employees doing a job that does not use their skillset

- Transportation
    - Poor workflow requiring unnecessary movement of material
    - Disorganized office with inconvenient access to necessities
    - Unnecessary movement of material. For example, keeping vaccinations in the front of the hospital versus in the treatment room

- Inventory

- Product on hand that exceeds customer demand
- Ordering excessive quantities of sales brochures

- Motion
    - Too many signatures required to approve an expense report
    - Inefficient layout for doctors to reach the treatment room
    - Walking the same route multiple times during one procedure

- Extra Processing
    - Multiple people being assigned to the same task
    - Bathing a dog three times when two suffices
    - Searching for an item incorrectly placed
    - Manually performing a process that could be automated[55]

By defining and eliminating the inefficiencies and defects, the structure of a system tightens up and focuses on delivering quality products or services.

In a culture of continuous improvement, team members examine daily processes and procedures. Team members begin looking at daily processes and procedures with the thought of how this system can improve. Continuous improvement cuts down on the amount of waste in a system or process and improves efficiency.

---

55 *Villanova University: Six Sigma Green Belt Online Textbook.* Tampa: Bisk Education, 2016, 6–8.

Through my experience of creating standard operating procedures for the team to follow, it eliminated repetition and created focused and productive workforces. According to Rachaelle Lynn a Senior Marketing Manager at Planview, "Processes that do not work can lead to numerous problems which consist of:

- Customers might complain about poor product quality or bad service
- Team members get frustrated
- Work might be duplicated or not completed at all
- Costs can increase
- Resources might be wasted
- Bottlenecks can develop, causing teams to miss deadlines"[56]

If everyone agrees upon a common goal and then develops, discusses, and follows the agreed upon processes and procedures, more collaborative workplaces can form.

CHECKLISTS, SHIFT CHANGES, AND TEAM HUDDLES

Streamlining processes and procedures by adopting best practices brings everyone to the same page. In veterinary practices, universal adherence to a set of standards and procedures ensures continuity of quality care through shift changes and turnover. Checklists streamline processes by clearly defining individual responsibilities and expectations, task by task.

---

56 Rachelle Lynn, "Why Is Process Improvement Important?" Planview, accessed May 27, 2020.

The clinic I worked at used various checklists. We used them for daily, weekly, and monthly responsibilities as well as training. The checklists seamlessly streamlined communication around major duties and also ensured patients received medications on time. Checklists allowed shift changes to go smoothly and created cross-functional teams by allowing one person to the next to know exactly where to pick up the next step in the day or the training process.

Team huddles serve as another tool that enhanced communication in veterinary practices. Team huddles allowed the team to gather and review all incoming patients for the day, procedures, drop-off appointments, sick appointments, employee and pet patient status, and share any additional updates the team had.

According to Registered Nurse (RN) Priscilla Di Vincenzo in the journal *Nursing2020*,

> Patients find that communicating with a cohesive team is much easier than trying to deal with multiple individuals walking in and out of their room on separate occasions. Effective communication between healthcare workers and patients can lead to shorter patient stays, increased patient satisfaction, improved flow of information, and more effective patient interventions.[57]

Team huddles at the beginning of the day and during shift changes allow patient care to continue without question.

---

57 Priscilla Di Vincenzo, "Team Huddles: A Winning Strategy for Safety," *Lippincott Nursing Center* 47, no. 7 (July 2017): 59–60.

EXAM ROOM PROTOCOL

In 2016, my medical director and I developed a streamlined approach to the Exam Room Protocol. Appointments made up the majority of time in a veterinary practice and depicted how the day would go. Among a group of leadership teams, we had the opportunity to participate in an eight-hour workshop led by a team of professionals from Elanco Animal Health. The workshop went over "The 4 Disciplines of Execution," also known as "4dx Methodology," by Franklin Covey and helped us choose a goal we wanted to work toward and implement in the hospital.

We used sticky notes to brainstorm project ideas and knew we wanted to choose a process that directly and indirectly impacted the following areas:

- Client/Patient wait time
- Client experience and education
- Completion of medical records
- Patient treatment times

Our workload increased substantially, and completing the medical records became an ongoing struggle. Our doctors came in on their off days to complete medical records because they didn't have enough perceived time to complete them during the pet's appointment. In an effort to amend this stressful situation for the team and for the clients, we decided to pilot the 4dx methodology to correct some of the shortcomings and stressors faced in the clinic. We picked a couple of top contenders during the workshop and went back to our team with them. As a result, all members of the team agreed that the client/patient wait times needed improvement.

Franklin Covey identifies the 4 Disciplines of Execution as follows:

1. Choose a Wildly Important Goal
2. Act on the Lead Measures
3. Keep a Compelling Scoreboard
4. Create a Cadence of Accountability[58]

Franklin Covey discusses the importance of a "WIG - Wildly Important Goal" in his book. A WIG impacts multiple systems and processes with the least amount of effort.[59] As a clinic, we decided that our WIG would be "To decrease the amount of time from check-in to check-out from seventy-five minutes to forty-five minutes by December 31, 2016." We chose this WIG because our client experience and patient journey throughout the hospital directly impacted the areas mentioned above.

The second discipline says to act on lead measures. Lead measures track the critical activities that drive the lag measure. The team directly influences the lag measure by acting on the lead measures. While a lag measure tells you if you've achieved the goal, a lead measure tells you the likelihood of achieving the goal.[60] In this process we defined our lead

---

58 Franklin Covey, "The 4 Disciplines of Execution," *Franklin Covey*, accessed October 6, 2020.
59 Ibid.
60 Chris McChesney, "Discipline 2: Act on the Lead Measures," *Franklin Covey*, accessed May 27, 2020.

measure as the amount of time each step in the process takes and the lag measure as the amount of time it takes from check-in to check-out. My medical director and I did a test run to measure how long it took each step in the process and used that as a baseline.

I created a simulation of timesheets for the staff to use to track the time required for each step of the process. We tracked a total of eighteen steps during the exam room process. Recording medical notes on paper and then typing them into the computer duplicated a step in the process. We eliminated the redundant step by ordering laptops for use during appointments. Assistants and technicians went into an exam room with a laptop to record the patient history directly into the medical record versus on paper and then entering it at a later time. By doing so, the amount of mental energy expended on remembering everything the client mentioned disappeared because the concerns could be entered directly into the medical record.

This eliminated at least ten minutes per appointment per day. On our team tracker we clearly identified our goal, each team member's role in the process, and highlighted the amount of time each step should take. Initially starting out, many expressed hesitations, but once everyone came together and worked toward this goal, it worked. In four months, client wait time decreased and the vets no longer came in on their days off to complete their medical records. We measured our client experience scores and they increased from an average of 85 percent across six categories to above 90 percent.

BEST PRACTICES

Implementing Franklin's Covey's, "4 Disciplines of Execution" in the practice led to the creation of best practices. Our efficiency increased, our processes streamlined, and we became a hospital focused on improving client education through the patient journey in the hospital. For the success of this initiative, we made sure to celebrate our successes along the way. When we met our goal, we had a team picnic at a local park and played kickball together. It created unity and camaraderie, and it helped the team see the importance of how focusing on one initiative at a time could make drastic improvements and impact more than one system in the hospital to alleviate the burden that has been on just one or two people. It became a shared responsibility, and our client experience scores improved as well as our patient care.

Focusing on designing a system structured around delivering consistent, quality care in a veterinary practice requires diligence, thought, and a lot of trial and error. Only by testing, refining, and then implementing and tracking can such systems be successful in a healthcare system that has so many components. Once you establish a system with clarity around processes and procedures, you can build a sustainable culture of continuous improvement.

You know the system works when the team works together as one unit. Your colleagues can predict your next step and step in to assist when needed. A functioning team reproduces quality work and wins at their jobs, and as a result, job satisfaction increases.

In my experiment with implementing a new exam room protocol, incorporating the EMR, and training the team, the overall morale of the team exponentially grew, we hired more staff, and everyone worked together like a well-oiled machine. Systems and processes in a hospital determine the efficiency in veterinary practices. These systems directly impact the patient, the staff, and the client.

Down the road, integration with insurance company software, pharmaceutical companies, and even the wellness plan became available. The EMR software became more of a collaboration tool, with evolved technologic functions. With all of the new and exciting features, came a set of challenges. I wondered how everybody would adapt to the new software, and which processes would need revamping to allow the hospital to flow seamlessly.

I've built the framework and established the importance of process improvement and having checks and balances. Having a framework as such allows teams to tackle bigger projects, for example, converting from paper to paperless patient records. Converting to an electronic medical record system in a hospital requires fine tuning and reevaluating almost every single process. My hospital went through the EMR conversion in early 2015 and required a plethora of training beforehand.

Every business should ask themselves, "What's *one thing* you can do this week to consolidate your tasks and eliminate all that is unnecessary?"

PART 4

PET CARE 2.0

CHAPTER 10

A VETERINARY PRACTICE IN 2030

When you work in the veterinary industry, you become the go-to resource when your friends have questions about their pets' health and habits. It's like having a walking, talking web search on your Facebook friends list. I've been tagged on many pet pictures and posts to conclude that my friends and my friends' dogs hate—and I mean hate—the Elizabethan collar. You may know it as "the cone of shame." It's that opaque or white flexible plastic shield that wraps around a dog's neck and head and makes him look like a big, sad snocone. Depending on the dog's size, the cone may be very big.

My dogs—Simba and Leo—absolutely hated the e-collar. They're so long and tall that an e-collar elongates their already lengthy body, creating less space in and out of the doorway. Simba would make us chase him around the house, and Leo would sit in once place for hours shaking vigorously because of his fear of the cone. As a pet owner, this absolutely disturbed my sisters and me. We thought, there must be an alternative. Simba and Leo's problem areas could be covered, we imagined, by something resembling a baby onesie—but big enough to fit a 110-pound German Shepherd.

So, we did a web search for "pet onesie" and discovered that somewhere in the world, a forward-thinking entrepreneur had not only perceived the need but conceived a solution. Two days later, the dogs were out of cones and in their onesies, and they loved them! Having eliminated the fearful object, Simba and Leo carried on with their normal activities, and we carried on with ours.

Pets all over the world have procedures and have to wear a cone of shame. Alternatives like pet onesies may not suit the needs of all of those pets, but this innovation helped Simba and Leo. This alternative, like others that have been invented, may work for a subset of the pet population.

Visionaries and entrepreneurs look into the world with a futuristic view and an innovative mindset. They assess areas of improvement and identify where they can make the greatest impact. Whether improving the lives of others, a product, a service, or company culture; visionaries and entrepreneurs persevere because of their dedication to their vision. Those who foresee the challenges in the industry and the long-term implications have the ability to cultivate best practices to alter and even reverse the effects.

> "Because we prepare new generations of veterinarians, academic veterinary medicine has a special responsibility when it comes to planning," said Dr. Michael Lairmore, American Association of Veterinary

Medical Colleges president. "Accelerating change has become the new status quo in our profession and we need leverage that builds and sustains success."[61]

According to The Futures Commission report, the following outcomes could result if veterinary professionals allow their future "to be dictated by events rather than taking a proactive approach to managing change":

- The current role of veterinarians as the leading experts in animal health care could be overtaken and their influence decreased over animal agriculture, science, research, public policy, and animal health generally.
- Alternative methods of veterinary care could displace veterinary clinicians as the primary option for animal health solutions.
- The profession could be no longer seen as an attractive career option for aspiring health care professionals.[62]

If veterinary professionals decide to become visionary individuals, they will be able to create a more sustainable future for the profession. The challenges the industry currently faces in regard to the suicide epidemic, compassion fatigue, burnout, and job satisfaction are key contributing factors to the upheaval in the profession. It's time to discuss solutions on how a culture of innovation, access to care, redefining job roles, continued learning, and developing a more sustainable industry model will impact the future of pet care.

---

61   AVMA, "Report Looks to Future of Veterinary Profession," *JAVMA News* (March 11, 2020).
62   Ibid.

CULTURE OF INNOVATION—WORK-LIFE HARMONY

The three major areas innovation can impact the lives of veterinary professionals are cultivating a schedule that promotes "work-life harmony," exploring the pros and cons of telemedicine, and enhancing communication with educational platforms.

My friend and colleague, Jackie Moffitt, shared how some days she worked thirteen hours straight, without being able to take a meal break. She worked overnight shifts in the emergency department, went home to rest, and then repeated the same thing the next day. Her schedule became so hectic that eventually she had to reassess how it was impacting her well-being in the long-term and adjust as needed to support a healthier work-life balance.

In an interview with Dr. Destiny Coleman, she shared a schedule made by her previous employer that allowed her to work her full-time hours and kept in mind employee wellness. "What I liked most about their schedule was that they only scheduled the veterinarians for thirty-three hours per week, accounting for the fact that you wouldn't be leaving on time."

They created a buffer to allow for that unpredictability in the schedule, and the remaining hours were made up with client calls backs, reviewing lab results, and completing medical records.

> Whereas, for example, my current job operates from ten o'clock in the morning to six thirty in the evening. I can probably count on my hand the number of times

that I left on time or before six thirty, meaning that I'm there until seven thirty or eight o'clock at night seeing these patients that nobody says no to. So, I liked that they actually built that into the schedule knowing that you don't really leave on time. It also meant that each doctor had a three-day workweek unless they worked the four-hour weekend shift, which was really nice. I never heard a doctor there complain about the schedule, and it's basically the only complaint I ever hear anywhere else.

Considering ways for creative scheduling can definitely address the burnout and exhaustion veterinary professionals face. Everyone has a different capacity, work ethic, and personal commitments. Creative scheduling can allow practice professionals to have flexibility in the workplace, while working their required hours.

CONTINUING EDUCATION AND LEARNING

As times change, so do the advances and standards of veterinary medicine. To keep up with the status quo, clinics should focus on continuing education and promoting it. Many veterinary practice professionals feel stuck in their positions, but due to personal limitations, they don't know how to continue advancing their careers. Creating different hierarchies of credentialing within the support staff would motivate employees and promote a culture of learning in hospitals.

A veterinarian sees all of the cases on the appointment book. The support staff may be involved in every other case, or a couple throughout the day. Veterinarians go through the same thing over and over and over each day, but if some of these systems were automated, it would help take off some of the pressure vets feel and in turn decrease the amount of burnout and compassion fatigue. Dr. Watson said, "You take this quotient of compassion fatigue and burnout off the table and you get a whole new veterinarian. They're much more creative and happier and have regained joy in their life."

Ashley, a licensed veterinary technician, shared how her clinic makes continuing education very important, which directly translates to the very high standard of medicine they practice.

> "Another thing to help veterinary support staff feel good about their jobs, would be the trust that veterinarians have in us," she says. "If they demonstrate that they want us to practice to the full extent of our license and allow us to learn things and do things that maybe not everyone else has the qualifications to do, that really helps with job satisfaction and not feeling stuck."

Veterinary laws and regulations change by state annually. Many of these changes directly impact what veterinary assistants and veterinary technicians can do under the supervision of a licensed veterinarian. As the laws continue to change, veterinary practices must promote advanced learning and credentialing of their assistants to avoid any repercussions.

In the veterinary profession, numerous assistants have the ability to perform the duties of a licensed technician, but new legislation restricted the use of their skills. For individuals who have technical skills but difficulty with academic curriculums, the Board of Veterinary Medicine should consider implementing different levels of credentialing certificates to allow skilled, long-term employees to use them to care for pet patients. I wouldn't want new legal regulations to discourage those people because their knowledge, skill, and experiences are incredibly valuable.

PET OWNER COMMUNITIES

Pet owner communities would also prove beneficial for the veterinary teams. Having a group of clinic clients gather into small groups based on breed, diseases, medical conditions, and any other questions that veterinarians and veterinary support teams triage would help pet owners when they learn about the diagnosis regarding the health of their pet.

By creating a clinic-based support group for clients, I foresee greater involvement and knowledge build among pet owners. Veterinary teams could create a network of pet owners for their clinic allowing discussion of common medical concerns and educate pet owners on what to expect with certain diseases promoting intellectual discussions when seeing the vet.

ACCESS TO CARE

In 2020, many industries nationwide have adopted broader remote work policies. In health care, conversations regarding telehealth and telemedicine have started happening. The human healthcare industry has been privy to and conducting telehealth consults for quite a few years now. However, the veterinary industry recently began to consider the impact of telemedicine and how the industry could benefit as a whole. Technologically the veterinary industry falls ten years behind current times, according to an article by Bob Lester in *Today's Veterinary Business* magazine.[63]

According to the AVMA, "**Telehealth** is the overarching term that encompasses all uses of technology to deliver health information, education or care remotely. Telehealth can be divided into categories based on who is involved in the communication. **Telemedicine** is a subcategory of telehealth that involves use of a tool to exchange medical information electronically from one site to another to improve a patient's clinical health status."[64] For years, veterinary professionals have triaged cases via telephone and communicated with clients and other industry professionals via email and text messages, however, not to the extent that could realize the benefits of telehealth.

Veterinary medicine poses some challenges when it comes to telemedicine because our patients cannot speak to us, and full physical exams allow veterinary professionals to complete a full patient assessment of the pets' body condition and overall physical health.

---

[63] Bob Lester, "We Can't Afford to Wait," *Today's Veterinary Business*, February, 2020.

[64] AVMA, "Veterinary Telehealth: The Basics," Telemedicine & Telehealth in a Veterinary Practice, accessed September 16, 2020.

Telemedicine could, however, impact:

- Follow-up appointments
- Lab consultations
- Detailed discussions with pet owners who like to learn more about the next steps for their pet
- Nutrition consults
- Prescription refills and recommendations via a home delivery system

Dr. Melanie Bowden says, "there's still a lot of work to be done in how we appropriately document phone call and email into medical records. I think it's also important to understand when a 'virtual' appointment is appropriate for example maybe checking a post-op incision, talking to a pet owner about chronic management of disease, or to discuss a new diagnosis and what is involved for treatment after the pet has been in for an exam and testing."

Vetsource, a pet health company, implemented a useful feature, *ScriptShare*. *ScriptShare* allows veterinarians to prescribe or recommend a medication through their website that then automatically sends the client an email with the doctor's medication recommendation and the prescription for the owner to fulfill the order right then and there. This avenue could prove successful during a virtual consultation with a vet when the pet needs prescription food or medications.

New generations of pet owners will do almost anything for their companion animal. Millennial pet owners outspend previous generations of pet owners. In a survey referred to by the American Animal Hospital Association (AAHA), 532 US millennial pet owners were asked[65]:

- What do you expect from your veterinary hospital experience?
- Where do you prefer to go for pet care?
- How do you know if the veterinarian loves your pet as much as you do?
- Why did you choose one veterinary hospital over another?
- What does a veterinary hospital do that earns your loyalty?
- What about a hospital makes you leave?

> The key finding: In order to win and keep millennial clients, veterinary hospitals need to provide professional, friendly care (also true of previous generations), *plus* great communication, which differs from previous generations: millennials grew up with and expect a very different kind of communication. Personal relationships are also especially important to millennial pet owners: 81 percent of millennials want their veterinarians to automatically know who they are when they call. Yet 72 percent of millennials said they've had to wait while their veterinarian looked up their account.[66]

To appeal to the current generation of pet owners, veterinary hospitals must build a relationship with them early

---

[65] Tony McReynolds, "What Millennial Pet Owners Want," AAHA, October 2, 2019.

[66] Tony McReynolds, "What Millennial Pet Owners Want," AAHA, October 2, 2019.

on. New generations of pet owners stay involved and interested in how to preserve the life of their pet and seek more communication. To keep up, developing a repository of common client educational material will assist veterinary professionals when their clients seek additional information regarding the health of their pet or disease conditions affecting their pet.

In an interview with Dr. Beecher Watson, a practicing veterinarian of over thirty-eight years and a previous clinic owner, shared his insight about what the future of veterinary medicine looks like in terms of wellness plans.

> A lot of households enroll in wellness plans offered by both private and corporate practices. The wellness plan works, and it's already been introduced. Taking that to the next step would be pairing it with telemedicine. Clients already pay monthly for the wellness plan, but what if we could take an exam or two to discuss the client concerns via a telehealth platform and assess pet health issues virtually? As veterinary professionals know, not every case is an emergency and with telehealth some of the non-emergent cases could be triaged more appropriately versus having to see every patient every time. This could help empower veterinary professionals by introducing a new component of their jobs, give veterinary nurses more autonomy, and take a load off of veterinarians and their support staff.

REDEFINING JOB ROLES

As technology evolves, the new generation becomes the largest population of pet owners, and the difficulty in retaining a consistent veterinary workforce, it's going to become crucial to leverage hospital teams. Dr. Watson suggested adopting a model similar to that of human health care, creating "Para-doctors," or different tiers of practice professionals similar to the model of physician assistants and nurse practitioners in the human medical field.

As technical positions increase in scope, veterinarians regain valuable time to focus on patient care or surgery and can collaborate with their veterinary technicians on follow-up care. If such a model existed, veterinary professionals would experience more flexibility and autonomy over their jobs. They would feel empowered to practice alongside the veterinarian, rather than obliged to wait for direction from the veterinarian. For this model to succeed, veterinarians and their support teams need to build trusting relationships and define job responsibilities and expectations early on.

Another option could be hiring contractors or consultants to ease the amount of stress on the staff, especially when it comes to training employees and developing educational material for clients and staff. For example, a pharmacy technician could be the point person to contact for medication refills and could coordinate with the doctor about authorized or declined refills. Rather than one person fulfilling numerous job responsibilities, assigning time, and building structure that allows individuals to focus on specific tasks would ensure thorough completion of tasks along with the day-to-day demands of the job.

Veterinary practices should also consider employing subject matter experts (SMEs) for various departments and job roles that currently fall under veterinary technicians. Advances in technology continue, but there's limited training in hospitals on how to operate equipment, enter medical records, and update or troubleshoot computers when needed. Hiring a technical person to operate all of the functional equipment could lead to less lost time when a system shuts down or when a backlog of records exists. This person could also focus on creating a repository of staff and client materials allowing for easy population of client friendly materials, which could make client communication more effective. We could add to the list of defined roles further by appointing a social media/marketing manager, behaviorist, medical coding specialist, and community outreach manager.

By redefining job roles and considering honing down on the job responsibilities associated with one position, we could decrease the amount of burnout in the industry and allow for more fluid communication between hospital teams.

TRANSPARENCY

Lastly, transparency.

Dr. Englar shared in a *DVM360* interview how human healthcare studies,

[show] how better communication leads to greater patient satisfaction, improved treatment adherence, increased retention and increased potential for referrals. When communication failed, patients said, they felt unheard and were less adherent to recommendations, less likely to show up for follow-up appointments and more likely to submit malpractice claims.[67]

In her pilot study looking at clients' perceptions of veterinarians' interpersonal skills, she identified two big gaps: transparency and unconditional positive regard. Defining transparency as "openness about medical procedures, procedural issues or errors," Dr. Englar encouraged attendees to think about ways this shows up:

- **Wait times and delays in diagnosis or treatment.** For example, explain that an emergency will delay a wellness appointment or that care may take a while.
- **Office hours and availability.** Calibrate expectations about what happens if a patient must be left receiving IV fluids, but your practice isn't staffed overnight.
- **Diagnostic unknowns.** Explain that test results aren't clear, and you just don't know yet.
- **Abilities and skill sets.** Assess what you feel capable of undertaking when it comes to procedures and treatment—and be honest. "At the end of the day, it's your license and up to you to feel comfortable," Dr. Englar said.
- **Medication errors.** Let pet owners know as soon as possible about wrong medications or improper doses.

---

67 Brendan Howard, "Transparency and Unconditional Positive Regard in Veterinary Medicine," *DVM360*, October 29, 2019.

"Don't just hope they never find out about it," Dr. Englar cautioned.[68]

Veterinary medicine remains a mystery for many until they enter the profession. More transparency about how many positions exist, the pay rates, and overall job expectations will lead to more open and honest communication as well as fairness. People appreciate transparency.

Job expectations and roles aren't always clearly defined because there are only five set hospital roles: veterinarian, veterinary technician, veterinary assistant, client care coordinator, and practice manager. If there was more definition to each of these job roles, whether clarity in what each role entails or the creation of more specialized roles, this would create greater understanding and accountability.

Another huge component of transparency, revolves around mental health. Mental health requires transparency, and veterinary professionals need a platform where they can talk openly about difficult cases and decisions to alleviate the escalation to serious mental health challenges. They need to share experiences with one another. When you're in an encouraging environment with people who care and are able to support each other, that's almost as important as the quality of medicine. Paying more attention to the people who do the work and taking care of them is a big deal to sustain a healthy workforce.

---

68   Brendan Howard, "Transparency and Unconditional Positive Regard in Veterinary Medicine," *DVM360*, October 29, 2019.

CHAPTER 11

THE EMOTIONAL WELL-BEING OF PETS

Some pets dislike visiting the veterinarian. Some pets emphatically dislike visiting the veterinarian. All pets require veterinary care to maintain good health, so even emphatically displeased pets must become patients, and Bear was one of the most emphatic patients we'd seen.

When Bear arrived at the veterinary clinic, he couldn't have stood more than a few feet tall. A Miniature Pinscher, he stood his ground in the exam room, nonetheless. When we entered the exam room, he let out a low growl befitting his namesake. Bear's fear threatened to impede his veterinary care because he snapped when we tried to touch him.

Then entered Andy Defayette, a behavior consultant and certified Professional Dog Trainer - Knowledge Assessed (CPDT-KA). Andy joined our veterinary practice in 2016. When he and Bear began their one-hour training sessions, Bear's owner would have to leave the room. As soon as his owner left, Bear no longer felt the need to protect her. He relaxed. Then Andy could get to work.

"I started off with him sitting in a corner and tossing him treats anytime he made movement towards me. By the second session, he came and sat in my lap. Each session helped him build a positive association with the vets office."

Bear still growls. However, he's much less reactive and has transformed to giving a warning signal when approached, rather than going into fight or flight mode. Now his owner can stay in the exam room with him. When Bear has his nails cut or blood drawn, we feed him a high value treat like cheese, and he tolerates it. "A lot of people didn't believe this would work. But when he came in for his blood draw, and he allowed us to do so, this was the biggest moment of his transformation, and I could say, 'See I told you so!'"

Ten years ago, fear-free practices weren't explicitly labeled, but several practiced low stress handling techniques to reduce the anxiety and fear a pet experienced at the veterinary hospital and others not so much. Labeling a pet as fractious or dangerous and using caution because the pet would usually bite indicated how the pet would behave in the clinic. A sticker system in place flagged charts to alert the veterinary staff of potentially nervous and aggressive patients. We payed less attention to the emotional experience of the patient and how we could change that. Pet owners and veterinary staff alike wanted to reduce the number of vet visits, have the nails done at all cost, and convenience preceded the emotional experience of that pet in the vet's office.

According to an article in 2014 by *DVM360*, the definition of fear, anxiety, and stress are as follows:

> Fear, by definition, is an emotion that induces an animal to avoid situations and activities that may be dangerous. The emotional response occurs when an animal perceives that something or someone is dangerous. The key word here is perceives. Anxiety is the anticipation of future danger that may be unknown, imagined, or real. It can result in physiologic responses similar to those associated with fear. While a certain amount of anxiety or fear may be adaptive in some situations, an animal that experiences fear or anxiety frequently, especially if unable to safely escape from fear-inducing stimuli, will begin to suffer from stress and its effects.[69]

At the time, struggling to restrain a patient or enlisting multiple assistants and technicians to help hold down a pet for a nail trim seemed normal. Sometimes scratches and bites occurred. Dr. Marty Becker, also known as "America's Veterinarian," stated in a 2016 interview, "Everything gets organized for the convenience of the veterinarian or the staff or to please the clients. Everything. But if you organize the practice to be compassionate to the animals first, you know as well as I do, you will be making a lot of changes."[70]

As time progressed and new industry practices surfaced, the idea of "low-stress handling" and "fear-free practices"

---

69 "The Physiologic Effects of Fear," *DVM360*, August 1, 2014.
70 Marty Becker, "Fear Free Pet Visits - How to Take the Pet Out of Petrified," *Fear Free, LLC,* January 14, 2016.

emerged. The emotional well-being of the pet and the case manager started to align, and proactive approaches alleviated the emotional distress both parties felt. Studies have shown that pets coming to a vet's office experience very high levels of fear, anxiety, and stress. I have experienced cats jumping off the table, running up the walls, and trying to attack veterinary personnel when taken out of their carriers. Similarly, difficult to handle dogs would buck, kick, lunge, and try to bite without warning and on top of that didn't allow safe placement of a muzzle.

Pets have become more important and integral members of the family. Pet patients require pet owners and veterinary professionals to become more intuitive about how they perceive certain situations. As a pet owner and a veterinary professional, it isn't okay with me that my pet or pet patient experiences fear, anxiety, and stress when visiting the veterinarian's office because these experiences will stay with that pet forever.

Pet behaviorists and trainers have started investing time in correcting behavioral issues and focusing on counterconditioning to create happy experiences. Helping a pet overcome their fears provides so much joy and happiness. It's a rewarding experience and allows the veterinary team, pet owners, and the people in the pets' lives to contribute to the solution, not the problem.

BEHAVIOR WAS A MYSTERY

Animals are intuitive and emotional creatures, and they process more than we know. Dogs specifically have been bred to adapt to the social nature of humans. According to Joey Turner from the Global Animal Foundation, "The average dog understands about 165 words and has the smartness of a two-year-old human, but the emotional development of a teenager."[71] The care of a pet begins at home and continues at a veterinary clinic. Both the pet owner and the veterinarian need to partner together and take into consideration not just the physical well-being of a pet but also the emotional well-being and focus on ways to create positive emotional experiences for the pet for the duration of their lives.

Andy's previous experiences as a Behavior Buddies Manager consisted of a training curriculum on how to introduce nervous dogs to the daycare environment. He spent half of a shift training other team members and half of a shift introducing new dogs to the daycare environment. The process required time, patience, and trust. Introducing a dog to a completely foreign and new environment could make or break their experience and ability to continue coming to a daycare.

When Andy joined our team, he began transforming our practice to focus on low-stress handling by taking into consideration the emotional response of a pet and creating a positive association for the pet with the vet's office. Andy stated,

> The level of fear in a daycare is almost identical to that of a new dog visit to the vet. When I began at the clinic, behavior appeared like a strange, mysterious science. I didn't walk in and think that it was a bad place for our

---

71 Joey Turner, "Dogs: Emotionally Intelligent as Teenagers." *Global Animal*, accessed June 2, 2020.

patients, but at the same time no one could point out the things that we had done right to make good relationships with the pets, or what we had done wrong to make the vets office a fearful place for some of the patients. The two questions my colleagues asked me when I arrived for my first day were, "What are we doing right?" and "What can we change?"

Andy focused on enhancing positive handling techniques and modifying other techniques that needed improvement in the clinic. He did this through staff training, education, one-on-one consults with pet owners, and private sessions with the pets. This allowed veterinary team members to perceive situations as a pet would. The questions that employees started asking themselves were:

- Was a doctor in a white coat scary?
- What loud noises startled a cat and how could we remove them?
- Were pheromone sprays, behavior management products, and therapeutic pharmaceuticals used appropriately?

All of these components and awareness about how a pet perceived human interaction became crucial in the movement toward low-stress vet visits.

Andy taught our staff to approach pets with a conscious mindset—to consider the experiences of a nail trim or blood draw from a pet's perspective. As a practice, we made considerate approaches to stop pushing pets beyond their comfort zones. Instead, we strove to create positive associations. If a pet didn't tolerate a nail trim today, we would utilize high-reward treats (usually peanut butter or some Cheez Whiz). If that didn't work, we would try and do one paw at a time. If that didn't work, then we would prescribe behavior management products or therapeutic pharmaceuticals to decrease the pet's anxiety and fear.

HOLISTIC APPROACH

Similarly, Dr. Julie Potter, a practicing veterinarian since 1995, applies a more holistic approach when examining patients. In this chapter the word "holistic" refers to veterinary practices that put the "whole pet" first and value the pet's emotional well-being as much as its physical well-being. Dr. Potter develops relationships with her patients to better understand them.

It wasn't always this way. Before adopting a holistic approach, Dr. Potter struggled with time. Her exams ran over their appointment times and she experienced frequent back-ups when completing her medical records. In a recent interview, Dr. Potter shared, "Exams take time. Building relationships with not just the pet owner but with the patient take time, and I didn't have enough time to do so. I was constantly criticized or hauled along to complete my appointments in a 15- or 20-minute window, which may not have been enough time for my patient to become comfortable with me."

The increasing demand of seeing an "x" number of patients in an "x" amount of time really shook her moral compass. She didn't want to push the animals, and she wanted to make sure she performed thorough examinations. With low-stress handling and creating a positive patient experience, time limited how much could be accomplished.

So how do we do this, and how can we make sure to continue building on considering the patient as a whole, the physical and emotional parts? Dr. Potter suggested gaining feedback from clients about how prior visits went, as they could provide valuable information for future vet visits. Understanding our pet patients at a personal level and using tools and techniques to support this initiative can reduce stress and increase enjoyment for those involved.

Fear Free Pets, LLC has launched an entire curriculum educating veterinary practice professionals on how to create fear-free veterinary visits. A few of the most successful fear-reducing techniques I have learned and seen work were using pheromone sprays and diffusers. These especially worked during feline exams. Another method used to reduce fear and anxiety in a pet patient were high-value treats. High-value treats distracted dogs from focusing on the unknown and focusing on the yummy treat. We also did brief exams or treatments outside for pets who resisted entering the clinic.

Key components of becoming a fear-free practice or certified individual consist of implementing daily fear-free techniques as mentioned above. They involved taking the time with the pet and having easy access to pheromone sprays, treats, and toys. To become fear-free certified, visit fearfreepets.com, an initiative started by Dr. Marty Becker.

MAKE THE PET OWNER PART OF THE EXPERIENCE

Visiting the vet isn't something pet parents should do once a year, rather five to six times a year to build a relationship. To enhance the pet patient experience, clinic personnel should invite pet parents to drop by with their pets for non-visits, such as coming by for a treat and to say hi. Food and medication pickups create opportunities to familiarize a pet with the clinic and socialize with the staff. These small steps can help a patient build positive associations with a vet clinic and the people working there. Practices and even pet owners should invest in this type of desensitization, counterconditioning, and forming relationships to decrease the environmental triggers that contribute to a stressful situation.

Adopting a conscious mindset, approaching pet care holistically, building relationships—these efforts do require an investment of time and money, but the return on investment is immeasurable. My nerves involved when working with an aggressive or fearful pet, subsided by adopting this mindset. Learning that a pet is fearful and working on ways to alleviate the fear, helped me use alternative methods when interacting with the nervous pets. I had alternative, effective methods of working with anxious animals I could use in these situations. The job satisfaction would go up because the physical human body wouldn't feel as much pain, and pets wouldn't feel scared or restricted when having medical treatments done.

Pet care should be a partnership between the veterinary staff and the pet owners. If the veterinarian says, "Hey we're going to try and do this," then follows through, it will work. But if there's any question of focused low-stress and fear-free visits, then it may be difficult. Behavior should be treated as a medical concern, and a treatment plan should be worked up for patients who have unpleasant emotions associated with vet visits. Considering the emotional well-being of pets has started to become more commonplace, and as an industry, continuing working toward this trend will lead to better patient visits and emotional responses to the veterinary team from the pet patient.

CHAPTER 12

THE FUTURE OF PET OWNERSHIP

Pets, like people, experience emotional trauma. We underestimate the fear and trauma rescue pets experience as they're shuffled from shelter to shelter, foster home to foster home. The implications can play out in their behavior for the rest of their lives. Sometimes, however, love can heal.

In 2020, my husband, Sunny, and I decided to foster a sweet, gentle German Shepherd dog for a couple of weeks. When he arrived from a high kill shelter, he was anxious, in poor body condition, and—weighing in at only forty-three pounds—severely underweight. If you're familiar with the German Shepherd breed most weigh a minimum of fifty-five to sixty pounds.

He had also lost his back right leg at some point in his life, but he carried himself with such exuberant joy that he quickly became the talk of our neighborhood. Everyone was drawn to him. He was a heartworm disease survivor with a big heart that craved a human to love. He was, in a word, resilient.

On his first night in our home, our foster friend laid by my side all night. He slept deeply, as though a heavy weight had been lifted off his chest, and he could finally rest. The next day I took him in for a grooming appointment to have his undercoat brushed out and his dull coat freshened up. The smile on this boy's face said everything, as if he'd never been bathed before. The gratitude emanated from his heart, and he relaxed.

He believed he would one day find his forever home. He kept fighting. That's where his name came from. His current owner, a very good friend of mine, Felicity, named him Miles because of the many miles he traveled throughout his life to find his permanent home. Luckily for Miles, Felicity extended her arms and welcomed him into her home. She continues to listen to him and provide him with all of the love, support, and comfort he needs to overcome his fears.

He greatly feared his human leaving and thunderstorms. He would panic and shake vigorously in one spot for minutes on end. Miles began presenting some of these concerns within a few weeks of his arrival. Felicity understood he had a rough life and the difficult situations he had been in. She gravitated toward Miles immediately and let him tell her he needed a patient owner. He needed time to learn that she would always come back. He needed time to learn that he could one day be fearless during storms.

The power of patience, love, and compassion can change the way another being experiences the world. Miles, you have taught me how many pets there are like you, with no place to call home. Together we can make a difference in the lives of pets in similar situations and provide them with the same compassion and understanding they need to overcome difficult situations. Miles reinforced the unconditional love dogs have to give, and the loyalty they have toward their humans no matter any circumstance.

Miles introduced me to the world of organized pet rescue. Most rescue groups operate with volunteers who share a common desire to help animals in unfortunate situations. The need is great, often greater than a volunteer-run, donation-reliant group can accommodate, however passionate its members may be. Limited resources and an overload of animals in need can leave even the most dedicated pet rescuers stretched too thin to provide the care, training, socialization, and assessment to effectively prepare a pet for placement.

As pet ownership becomes more common, and millennials prefer to adopt a pet before starting a family, it's imperative that we begin educating new pet owners on what to expect when owning a pet. Owning a pet requires more than fulfilling basic care needs. As pet owners, we need to take the time to understand our pets on a deeper, more intuitive level to understand them as a whole. Pets have so much love to give and learn from us, but they also have a lot to teach us about unconditional love, happiness, and intuition or that "gut feeling."

THE EVOLUTION OF PET OWNERSHIP

Starting out as a first-time pet owner in 2003 with Heidi, to a second-time pet owner with Simba and Leo, my mindset about pet ownership changed dramatically. The amount of knowledge I gained in eleven years of having Heidi amazes me. I learned responsibility for another living being who depended on me. I kept track of the number hours she stayed home alone. I exercised her and played games that would stimulate her mind. Brain games for dogs help them continue growing intellectually. I developed an unbreakable bond with her, and she became my soulmate. If she wasn't feeling well, I started to pick up on cues indicating changes in her behavior and she did the same.

Reports show that pet parents bring home a pet because pets teach children how to be responsible and nurturing while providing companionship and love. "According to parents, children maintain high levels of daily involvement in caring for and playing with family pets as the children grow from preschoolers to teens."[72] As this bond evolves, people form an attachment to their pets, and continue to evolve and learn about unconditional love and care.

In the primitive time period, the relationship between humans and animals was that of a hunter and a prey. Hunters primarily used animals as a source of food and skin for clothing. About twelve thousand to fourteen thousand years ago, the primitive people first domesticated a wolf, the ancestor to dogs. People discovered wolves submitted to humans and could be trained. However, modern day pet ownership came about in the nineteenth century as people learned more about animals and began developing relationships with them.[73]

---

[72] Pavol Prokop and Christoph Randler, *Ethnozoology: Animals in Our Lives* (Amsterdam: Elsevier, 2018), ch. 23.
[73] "The Evolution of Pet Ownership," Pedigree, accessed September 10, 2020.

In light of how pet ownership has evolved, pet advocacy groups have also formed. In support of pet advocacy efforts to protect animal rights, legislators have passed laws punishing those who enacted animal abuse or cruelty. "With the President signing the Preventing Animal Cruelty and Torture (PACT) Act, animal cruelty is no longer just unacceptable, but now illegal," said Representative Ted Deutch. "We can now finally say that animal abuse poses as a federal crime in the United States. Americans have long stood in support of animal welfare protections, and now our national laws reflect these values."[74]

PET OWNERSHIP IS ON THE RISE

Pet ownership correlates with certain positive physiological measures, such as lower blood pressure, serum triglycerides, and cholesterol levels, which ameliorate the cardiovascular effects of stress. Furthermore, close relationships with pets positively influence oxytocin release; one of the body's "feel good" chemicals and also plays a role in social bonding.[75]

Those who have interacted with pets and have experienced an upsetting time—the feeling of being lost, lonely, or frustrated—have witnessed their companion animal run to

---

[74] Emily Ehrhorn, "Extreme Animal Cruelty Can Now Be Prosecuted as a Federal Crime," *The Humane Society of the United States*, November 25, 2019.

[75] Gail F. Melson and Audrey H. Fine, *Handbook on Animal-Assisted Therapy: Theoretical Foundations and Guidelines for Practice* (Amsterdam: Elsevier, 2010), ch. 12.

comfort them. As an animal's natural instinct, they come to you providing comfort when you're upset. "Animals rely heavily on their intuition for survival and it is at the core of every living being. [Intuition serves as an animal's] first resource, where humans learn to use cognitive abilities and subsequently have paid less attention to and even ignored their intuition."[76] As we learn more about all that animals have to offer, and as companionship with animals rises, the mindset of pet ownership evolves.

Many new pet parents yearned for companionship. Being quarantined and isolated from loved ones, pets provided comfort during the COVID-19 pandemic in 2020. Now that many people have the ability to work remotely, it seems like the perfect time to adopt a pet. Pet owners have time to train and housebreak a new pet. As a result of increased adoptions during the pandemic, veterinary clinics have seen plenty of new pet patients. Overwhelmed veterinary clinics feel like they are drowning in the number of appointments seen per day. Even the appointment schedules remain fully booked several days out, with surgery scheduled almost one month out. Veterinary emergency clinics have also witnessed up to eight-hour wait times, which is unheard of in the veterinary field.

People will do more than they once did to preserve the human-animal bond with their pets and as a result have been spending more money on pet care. Pets no longer reside as barn animals, farm animals, or a piece of property. They are

---

76 "Intuitive Connections with Animals," *Animal Intuition* (blog), accessed September 10, 2020.

members of our families, and pet parents will do more than they have ever done before to preserve the lives of their pets.

TRAINING

One of the interesting components of pet ownership, or pet parenting, revolves around building a structured foundation to support our pets as they became integrated members of our families. Working with a credible trainer helps control problematic behaviors such as chewing the furniture and pulling on a leash. Finding ways to socialize dogs will help them acclimate to new environments and build their confidence. Training helps develop a good relationship between you and your pet. It allows for mutual trust and respect between both parties.

I was only thirteen years old when we took Heidi to her puppy classes, and I didn't understand the importance of continuing her training past the puppy years. I learned the importance of training Heidi to "heel" and "come" through the years of her life and made sure these were behaviors my dogs, Simba and Leo, learned. Being pulled on a leash by a large dog didn't fit the definition of fun. I learned by encouraging good behavior early on, it would alleviate a lot of frustrations later in life.

In some cases, pet parents end up adopting a pet who becomes aggressive over time, and managing those behaviors becomes difficult. In this case, desensitizing the pet to triggers and creating positive associations with what's scary helps alleviate the level of reactivity. Not only can an aggressive pet pose danger to strangers, but they can also become a problem in the home. Paying attention to cues and working with your pet to resolve them leads to a more fulfilling life for the pet and the pet owner.

Training helped long-time pet owner Barbara Tribbie develop a stronger bond and connection with her pets. "When I first took my kitty to the vet in 1982 (in Norfolk) I got her out of her kennel, and she reached around my neck with her paws and didn't want to let go! She was very scared being there," Mrs. Tribbie said, in an interview.

> I hope all vets have become more compassionate with the animals as time has passed. My pets are my family, they always have been. The years have helped and the training available for dogs also helps with bonding. I take a more personal responsibility when it comes to their care. It's my way of giving back so to speak for the ones who aren't as lucky to have a good pet life.

Good news, Mrs. Tribbie. Our team's access to educational resources and research on animal behaviors has increased over the years, supporting positive reinforcement and conditioning techniques.

FINANCIAL TOOLS TO HELP PET OWNERS BETTER CARE FOR THEIR PETS—PET WELLNESS PLANS

As pet ownership continues rising, pet owners must familiarize themselves on how to care for a pet and the cost of owning a pet. From the fixed costs, to the unexpected vet bills, owning a pet has become more expensive over the years. Many pet owners adopt a pet for companionship; however, they feel unprepared and alarmed when they find out how much everything a pet needs costs. According to a recent report from the American Pet Products Association, Americans spent $95.7 billion on their pets in 2019, which included pet food and treats, supplies, live animals, over-the-counter medication, and vet care.[77]

Finances around pet care are surprising to not just pet owners but even to veterinary professionals who work in clinic. The prices set by many veterinary hospitals take into consideration several factors. The cost of a service includes the complexity of the task, lab costs, the amount of time a service takes, and the number of people and expertise needed to deliver the service. Pet owners may benefit from learning about all of the components that comprise the cost of a veterinary service. Veterinary staff receive pay on an hourly rate or a salary, and the money that comes into the hospital is divided up between operating costs and expenses. All of the operating costs ensure the hospital operations continue and allow for the continuation and advancement of veterinary medicine.

To prepare for some of the costs associated with owning a pet, pet wellness plans and insurance options are great tools to mitigate the financial risk associated with pet ownership. It gives pet owners peace of mind. In the event of an emergency, they have the support of an insurance plan to make

---

[77] David Weliver, "The Annual Cost of Pet Ownership: Can You Afford a Furry Friend?" *Money Under 30*, Modified July 7, 2020.

appropriate health decisions for their pet. Awareness about pet health insurance can help pet owners and veterinary professionals overcome challenges related to the cost of pet care. Pet owners can rest assured if their pet comes up with an illness or injury, the pet insurance will cover a certain amount of the treatment based on their policies and provisions. The amount of conversations around cost could be decreased and a reduction in the amount of stress around financial planning and spending for owners would decrease. The number of conversations around cost would decrease and so would the stress around financial planning and spending for pet owners.

Wellness plans and insurance plans differ in that wellness plans usually consist of preventative care for a pet, whereas insurance plans cover a portion of the cost for illness. With numerous pet insurance companies out there, it can be difficult to decide which one to choose. When looking at pet insurance plans, take into consideration the pet breed, the monthly cost, the amount of the deductible, the waiting period, and if there's a cap on the payout amount for medical conditions. Many pet insurance companies also have breed-specific exclusions, so be sure to read the fine print when choosing which option is best for you.

I can say from my personal experience, not having pet insurance for Heidi put me in a position of having to take out the majority of my savings to save her life. She had a malignant splenic mass that required an ER visit, numerous blood transfusions, hospitalization, emergency surgery, pain medications, and fluids that amounted to just under $10,000. When she was a puppy, I wasn't aware pet insurance existed. Had I known it did, I would have enrolled her in a protection plan from the start. The advantage of signing up for pet insurance early in a pet's life is that plans rarely cover treatment deemed to result from a preexisting condition or chronic illness. I highly recommend that any current or future pet owners look into pet insurance options. Nowadays, some employers even offer this benefit as part of an employment package.

Needless to say, no questions arose when I enrolled my dogs—Simba and Leo—in pet insurance plans. Having pet insurance allows me to pursue more intensive diagnostics and treatment without which I may not have been able to. Having the security of knowing that my pet insurance company will be there to help me with the financial costs provides me with the mental piece of not having to worry about money at the expense of my pet's life. Pet insurance helps me ensure my pet's longevity. Pet owners may not have enough knowledge about pet insurance, but it can help tremendously to overcome the stress of the cost associated with pet care.

SIGNING UP FOR PET OWNERSHIP EDUCATIONAL COURSES

There's so much to learn when owning a pet, and to assist pet owners with this role, pet health companies have started offering owner specific educational courses and reading material. They also provide resources regarding how to brush your pet's teeth, certain disease conditions, and breed specific information. There are many articles online by accredited veterinary journals such as the *AVMA, Life Learn, AAHA*, and more pertaining to specific food and medications made by pet healthcare companies such as Zoetis, Merck, Royal Canin, and Hills. These resources can help pet owners learn more about the health of their pet.

Veterinary offices also have access to a plethora of educational materials. These can be built into a repository around the most frequently asked questions on veterinary topics pertaining to a pet's healthcare status and be shared with clients. Pet owners should also consider familiarizing themselves with how to promote a fear-free environment at home. By doing so, pet owners can learn how to create a stress-free environment at home and control anxiety early on to help the pet live a happy and healthy life.

One thing I hope will happen is the use of pet owner webinars, and more educational videos for pet owners to view at home on how to take care of their pets when they can't get to the vet. The rise in pet ownership compared to the number of vet professionals seems to have spiked at a ratio that's hard to keep up with. Educating pet owners about common injuries and illnesses that can be cured at home via telehealth visits, will help reduce the backlog of veterinary visits. This may also alleviate the burden veterinary professionals face with the excessive surplus of appointments given the situation that has arisen with COVID-19.

CONCLUSION

Pets mean family. Pet owners want their pets to live forever and so do veterinary professionals. What started off as an endeavor to eradicate a Cattle Plague, developed into a multibillion-dollar industry focused on saving the lives of domesticated pets, as well as caring for farm animals. The majority of domesticated animals remain small animals, and the veterinary teams who provide for them talented professionals.

Western Animal Clinic interviewed Dr. Fricchione who points out,

> Our pets bring more to our lives than it may appear. In addition to love, companionship, and the emotional connection that humans crave, we actually change our actions when owning a pet. "We do best medically and emotionally when we feel securely attached to another, because we're mammals and that's the way we've evolved. We feel especially secure with dogs and cats because of the unconditional love they provide. No matter what you do or say, your dog or cat accepts you and is attached to you. Taking care of a dog or a cat can provide a sense of purpose and a feeling of validation when you wake up or come home and there's someone who's happy to see you."[78]

By adopting these recommendations, we can decrease the emotional burden on veterinary staff. We can decrease the number of times the veterinary team delivers heart-breaking news because pet owners can become educated about early disease detected through wellness plans. We can help pet owners help their pets. Together we can positively impact and transform the veterinary profession for the future.

---

78 "What Does Your Pet Mean to You?" Western Animal Clinic, December 19, 2017.

ACKNOWLEDGMENTS

From the bottom of my heart, all I feel is gratitude to have had you all by my side throughout this journey. Without all of you, I wouldn't have had the courage to continue writing and sharing this story. You reaffirmed the need for this book in the veterinary space, and I am so proud to have gone through this journey with all of you.

To all of my readers, thank you for joining me on this journey and for encouraging the larger community to help transform the future of the veterinary industry.

To all of my beta readers and early supporters, thank you for believing in this crazy idea long before everyone else did. This book would truly not be here without you!

To my fabulous family and friends, thank you for the unconditional love and support. You continued to push me to keep going when the very thought of writing felt daunting. Our discussions sparked new talking points for this book throughout the journey and gave me even more perspective to make this book the best it could be.

To my interviewees, thank you for being so generous with your time and working my interview requests into your busy schedules. Thank you for sharing your passion and knowledge with me and so many others along the way.

To those who helped me with promoting my book, thank you for taking the time to speak with me and spread awareness about my book.

To those whom I've worked with over the years in the veterinary space, thank you for always supporting and encouraging me in developing my skills and helping me grow into who I am now. I have learned so much from each and every one of you and admire all that you do for our pet patients and for each other. Those experiences have enabled me to develop a broader perspective about the industry and life in general.

Finally, a huge thank you to Eric Koester, the teams at the Creator Institute and the entire New Degree Press team for bringing my book to fruition. To my editors, Cortni Merrit and P. Richelle White, thank you for coaching me through this journey of writing my debut book and taking my book from "good" to "great"! You never stopped believing in me, and I will forever cherish the time spent working with you in making my dream come true.

Thank you!

FAMILY, COLLEAGUES, FRIENDS, AND SUPPORTERS

Deepti Taneja
Vijay Taneja
Reema Taneja
Mahima Taneja
Sunny Gupta
Alexandria Murphy
Ali Family
Alisia Smith-Rucker
Amandeep Saini
Amar Oak
Amber Bunch
Amira Meawad
Amy RedPath
Amy Younger
Anam and Josh Gannett
Andrea Honig
Andrew Defayette
Anisha Jain
Anna Defayette
Anuj Patel
Anuj and Tiffany Prashar
Apoorva and Arth Patel
April DelaCruz Sabado
Arjun Chudasama
Asha Patel
Ashlea and Ryan Creegan
Ashley Gray
Ashley Yoder
Astha Naral
Ava Ataee
Azadeh Chegini
Baburao Samala
Barbara Tribbie
Barka Farheen
Batra Family
Dr. Beecher Watson
Bethany Huheey
Bhavna Tailor
Brooke and Robert Miller
Bruce Leftwich
Candice Bhatia
Cara and Cody Majer
Dr. Christine and Jeff Santiago
Claire Votaw
Courtney and Scott Gliosca
Crissy Kibic
Cristhian M. Parra
Crystal and Sandy Benton
Crysty Erwin
Daniel Vermillion
Denise Caso
Destiny Coleman
Dev Rawat
Diane Johnson
Diane and Daniel Polsby
Dinesh Tandon
Dode Family
Donald Lavanty
Donna Huber
Donna Watson
Dustin Cannon
Eliseo Silva
Elizabeth Troncoso
Dr. Elizabeth Van Sickle
Erika Ambrosino
Ethan Ngo
Felicity Boyer
Gennifer Davis
Gharai Family
Gina Matharoo
Gina Stoyle
Gloria Britton
Gupta Families
Dr. Hayley Sherwood

Henry Metz
Iqra Kapadia
Jacqueline Le
Jacqueline Moffitt
Jain Family
Jason Dews
Jason Key
Jay Kershenstein
Jenn Zakarian
Jennifer Scott
Dr. Jessica Magnotti
Joan Wu
Jonathan Stoffer
Judy Jackson
Dr. Julie Potter
Julie Stevans
Jutka Terris
Karisa Dominguez and Ryan Gearheart
Katen Goyal
Katie and Chris Forsland
Kayla Donovan
Khalid Beikas
Kimberly Weilnau
Kochhar Family
Lana McMahon
Dr. Lance Roassa
Lauren Copeland
Lauren Corbin and Jerry Owens
Lauren Eskew
Laya Muralidharan
Leah Aguilar
Liza Hashim
Lorrie Stiles
Lynn and Brent Neubauer
Mangat Family
Manjit and Devika Singh
Mariam Ahmed
Maricela Jimenez-Moreno
Mark Smith
Mary and Jason O'Gray
Dr. Mary Jo Palmer
Mary Nardelli
Dr. Meenakshi Shah Kalra
Mehra Family
Dr. Melanie Bowden
Dr. Melinda Crowley
Michael Gomez
Dr. Michael Haas
Michelle Righenzi
Moin Uddin
Natalia Almada
Nayak Family
Nechel Family
Negi Family
Nicole Tawney
Nitin Kedia
Noah Black
Palak Patel
Patty Shama
Purohit Family
Raj Varma
Rajiv Shah
Rani Kumar
Rashi and Sandeep Sharma
Ravi Dhar
Rebecca Campoverde
Renee Wells
Rick McMahill
Ridge Pearson
Riley and Christopher LeNoir
Riya Parikh
Saif Mirza
Sally Stroup
Dr. Sandhya Pal Jopp
Sanjoy Tandon
Sapna Grover
Sara and Imtinan Ullah

Sarah McMillan
Sarah Newhart
Sasha Bentley
Satish More
Dr. Shabnam and David Prophet
Shafiq Ahmad
Sharmila Tandon
Shawheen Dasti
Shreya Jha
Shweta Agarwal
Simran Sehgal
Stephanie and Carlos Cruz
Steve Gunderson
Sydney Day
Taneja Family
Dr. Tannetje Crocker
Tanya Moore
Ted Carney
Tess Boyer
Tulsi and Sachin Bhargava
Dr. Veronica Jarvinen
Virginia Bianco-Mathis
Witek Family
Zenya and Mazhar Nadiawala

APPENDIX

INTRODUCTION

Chan, Melissa. "Veterinarians Face Unique Issues That Make Suicide One of the Profession's Big Worries." *Time*, September 12, 2019. https://time.com/5670965/veterinarian-suicide-help/.

Delaney, Janet. "Veterinarians Are Killing Themselves. An Online Group Is There to Listen and Help." *NPR*, September 7, 2019. https://www.npr.org/2019/09/07/757822004/veterinarians-are-killing-themselves-an-online-group-is-there-to-listen-and-help.

Filipo, Michael S. "Special Report: Auburn-CDC Study Examines Frequency and Means of Suicide among Veterinary Professionals." *JAVMA*, September 1, 2019. https://www.avma.org/news/press-releases/special-report-auburn-cdc-study-examines-frequency-and-means-suicide-among.

Fullerton, Emily. "How to Avoid Burnout in Veterinary Nursing." *Today's Veterinary Nurse*, 2019. https://todaysveterinarynurse.com/articles/final-thoughts-burnout-in-veterinary-nursing/.

Griffin, Brenda. "Working with Veterinarians." *University of Florida: College of Veterinary Medicine.* http://www.humanesociety.org/sites/default/files/archive/assets/pdfs/pets/feral-cats/working-with-a-vet.pdf.

Horton, Melissa. "Average Student Loan Debt for Veterinarians." *Lendedu*, November 27, 2019. https://lendedu.com/blog/average-student-loan-debt-for-veterinarians/.

Kramer, Mary H. "Veterinary Career Myths." *The Balance Careers*, June 25, 2019. https://www.thebalancecareers.com/veterinary-career-myths-125835.

Stephens, Stephanie. "Compassion Fatigue: 3 Steps to Setting Boundaries in Healthcare." *Health eCareers*, November 15, 2016. https://www.healthecareers.com/article/career/set-boundaries-heal-yourself-first.

TED. "Melanie Bowden: What Being a Veterinarian Really Takes." March 10, 2020, video, 19:04. https://www.youtube.com/watch?v=objP3E625X0&feature=youtu.be.

"What Your Veterinarian Needs You to Know about Compassion Fatigue andSuicide in the Veterinary Profession." *The Meowing Vet* (blog), September 10, 2018. Accessed April 1, 2020. http://themeowingvet.com/2018/09/10/what-your-veterinarian-needs-you-to-know-about-compassion-fatigue-and-suicide-in-the-veterinary-profession/.

CHAPTER 1

Fear Free Pets, LLC. "Fear Free Certification Program." Module 1 Fear Free Behavior Modification Basics at Fear Free, LLC. Accessed May 8, 2020. https://fearfreepets.com/courses/fear-free-certification-program/#l1-introduction.

CHAPTER 2

"An Era of Change: A Closer Look at Veterinary Education and Practice." *University of California*, 2015. https://www.ucop.edu/uc-health/_files/vet-med-an-era-of-change.pdf.

Bedford, Emma. "Number of Pet Owning Households in the United States in 2019/20, by Species (in Millions)." *Statista*, March 24, 2020. https://www.statista.com/statistics/198095/pets-in-the-united-states-by-type-in-2008/.

Hendrix, Michael. "Are Cities Going to the Dogs?" *City Journal*, October 8, 2019. https://www.city-journal.org/pet-ownership-over-children-cities.

CHAPTER 3

Burrington, Brad. "Changing Times, Changing Technology: Veterinary Medicine Over the Years." *Lucy Mackenzie Humane Society* (blog), Pet Hospital Veremedy, August 12, 2014. http://veremedy.com/2225/changing-times-changing-technology-veterinary-medicine-over-the-years/.

Cole, L. "A Quick History of Veterinary Medicine." *Canidae* (blog), November 4, 2014. https://www.canidae.com/blog/2014/11/a-quick-history-of-veterinary-medicine/.

Gamble, Molly. "5 Retail Principles for a More Effective Hospital Market Share Strategy." *Becker's Hospital Review*, April 3, 2013. http://www.beckershospitalreview.com/hospital-physician-relationships/5-retail-principles-for-a-more-effective-hospital-market-share-strategy.html.

Larkin, Malinda. "Pioneering a Profession: The Birth of Veterinary Education in the Age of Enlightenment." *JAVMA News*, (December 19, 2010). https://www.avma.org/javma-news/2011-01-01/pioneering-profession.

"Retrospective: A Brief History of Veterinary Medicine." *Oakland Veterinary Referral Services* (blog), September 27, 2019. https://www.ovrs.com/blog/history-of-veterinary-medicine/.

Soloman, Kristine. "14 Animals That Are Surprisingly Legal to Own as Pets in the US." *Business Insider*, October 4, 2019. https://www.businessinsider.com/animals-legal-pets-us-surprising-2019-10#the-majority-of-tigers-live-as-pets-not-in-the-wild-2.

"3 Ways Technology Has Changed." *University of Illinois at Chicago* (blog). Accessed March 9, 2020. https://healthinformatics.uic.edu/blog/3-ways-technology-has-changedhealthcare/#:~:text=A%20number%20of%20industry%20analysts,than%20it%20has%20ever%20been.

CHAPTER 4

Data USA. "Data USA: Veterinarians & Veterinary Technologists and Technicians." Accessed April 12, 2020. https://datausa.io/profile/soc/veterinarians?compare=veterinary-technologists-and-technicians.

Dicks, Michael. "Fixing the Veterinary Profession before It's Too Late." *VIN News*, May 13, 2019. https://news.vin.com/default.aspx?pid=210&Id=9049693&useobjecttypeid=10&fromVIN-NEWSASPX=1.

Insurance Information Institute. "Facts + Statistics: Pet Statistics." Accessed September 2, 2020. https://www.iii.org/fact-statistic/facts-statistics-pet-statistics#:~:text=in%20North%20America.-,Pet%20ownership%20in%20the%20United%20States,-Pet%20Products%20Association%20(APPA).

US Bureau of Labor Statistics. *College Enrollment and Work Activity of Recent High School and College Graduates Summary.* Washington, DC. Last modified April 28, 2020. https://www.bls.gov/news.release/hsgec.nr0.htm.

US Bureau of Labor Statistics. *Occupational Employment Statistics.* Washington, DC. Last modified July 6, 2020. https://www.bls.gov/oes/current/oes319096.htm.

US Bureau of Labor Statistics. *Veterinarians: Occupational Outlook Handbook.* Washington, DC. Last modified September 1, 2020. https://www.bls.gov/ooh/healthcare/veterinarians.htm.

US Bureau of Labor Statistics. *Veterinary Technologists and Technicians: Occupational Outlook Handbook*. Washington, DC. Last modified April 10, 2020. https://www.bls.gov/ooh/healthcare/veterinary-technologists-and-technicians.htm.

Velazquez, Jade. "How Can You Improve Mentorship in Your Clinic?" *Dr. Andy Roark*, March 3, 2016. https://drandyroark.com/can-improve-mentorship-clinic/.

CHAPTER 5

AVMA. "Veterinarian's Oath." AVMA Policies. Accessed May 21, 2020. https://www.avma.org/resources-tools/avma-policies/veterinarians-oath#:~:text=Being%20admitted%20to%20the%20profession,of%20public%20health%2C%20and%20the.

Holowaychuk, Marie. "Is Empathy Good or Bad for Veterinary Caregivers?" *LinkedIn*, June 19, 2019. https://www.linkedin.com/pulse/empathy-good-bad-veterinary-caregivers-marie-holowaychuk/.

Leffler, David. "Suicides among Veterinarians Become a Growing Problem." *The Washington Post*, January 23, 2019. https://www.washingtonpost.com/national/health-science/suicides-among-veterinarians-has-become-a-growing-problem/2019/01/18/0f58df7a-f35b-11e8-80d0-f7e1948d55f4_story.html.

Mathieu, F. "What Is Compassion Fatigue?" *Tend Academy*, 2019. https://www.tendacademy.ca/what-is-compassion-fatigue/.

Mayo Clinic. "Job Burnout: How to Spot It and Take Action." November 21, 2018. https://www.mayoclinic.org/healthy-lifestyle/adult-health/in-depth/burnout/art-20046642.

TED. "Melanie Bowden: What Being a Veterinarian Really Takes." March 10, 2020, video, 19:04. https://www.youtube.com/watch?v=objP3E625X0&feature=youtu.be.

CHAPTER 6

Bleich, Cory. "6 Major Benefits to Cross-Training Employees." *EdgePoint, LLC* (blog). https://www.edgepointlearning.com/blog/cross-training-employees/. "Emotional Intelligence." *Psychology Today*, 2020. https://www.psychologytoday.com/us/basics/emotional-intelligence.

Summers, Rachel. "How to Communicate Effectively with Your Team." *ProSky*, March 31, 2020. https://talkingtalent.prosky.co/articles/how-to-communicate-effectively-with-your-team.

"The Cost of Poor Communication." *SHRM*, 2013. https://www.shrm.org/resourcesandtools/hr-topics/behavioral-competencies/communication/pages/the-cost-of-poor-communications.aspx#:~:text=David%20Grossman%20reported%20in%20%E2%80%9CThe,communication%20to%20and%20between%20employees.

CHAPTER 7

Hasan, Syed Fazal E., Ian Lings, Larry Neale, and Gary Mortimer. "The Role of Customer Gratitude in Making Relationship Marketing Investments Successful." *Journal of Retailing and Consumer Services* 21, no. 5 (September 2014):788–96. https://www.sciencedirect.com/science/article/abs/pii/S0969698914000848?via%3Dihub.

Smith, Jeremy A. "Five Ways to Cultivate Gratitude at Work." *The Greater Good Science Center at the University of California, Berkeley*, May 16, 2013. https://greatergood.berkeley.edu/article/item/five_ways_to_cultivate_gratitude_at_work.

CHAPTER 8

AVMA. "New Hire Mentoring Programs." Career Articles. Accessed September 15, 2020. https://www.avma.org/education/tips-veterinary-jobseekers/new-hire-mentoring-programs.

Glassdoor. "How to Identify and Develop Soft Skills." Accessed September 15, 2020. https://www.glassdoor.com/blog/guide/develop-soft-skills/. Indeed. "Soft Skills: Definitions and Examples." Accessed September 15, 2020. https://www.indeed.com/career-advice/resumes-cover-letters/soft-skills.

Tait, John T., et al. "American Animal Hospital Association: Mentoring Guidelines." *Trends Magazine*, May/June 2008. https://www.aaha.org/globalassets/02-guidelines/mentoring/mentoring-guidelines.pdf.

Tricarico, Erica. "Why Vulnerability Is Vital in Veterinary Medicine." *DVM360*, August 30, 2020. https://www.dvm360.com/view/why-vulnerability-is-vital-in-veterinary-medicine.

CHAPTER 9

Covey, Franklin. "The 4 Disciplines of Execution." *Franklin Covey*. Accessed October 6, 2020. https://www.franklincovey.com/Solutions/Execution/4-disciplines.html.

Di Vincenzo, Priscilla. "Team Huddles: A Winning Strategy for Safety." *Lippincott Nursing Center* 47, no. 7 (July 2017): 59–60. https://www.nursingcenter.com/journalarticle?Article_ID=4198202&Journal_ID=54016&Issue_ID=4198035.

Lynn, Rachelle. "Why Is Process Improvement Important?" Planview. Accessed May 27, 2020. https://www.planview.com/resources/articles/why-process-improvement-important/.

McChesney, Chris. "Discipline 2: Act on the Lead Measures." *Franklin Covey*. Accessed May 27, 2020. https://www.franklincovey.com/the-4-disciplines/discipline-2-act.html.

Toussaint, John. S. and Correia, Kathryn. "Why Process Is US Healthcare's Biggest Problem." *Harvard Business Review*, March 19, 2018. https://hbr.org/2018/03/why-process-is-u-s-health-cares-biggest-problem.

Villanova University: Six Sigma Green Belt Online Textbook. Tampa: Bisk Education, 2016.

CHAPTER 10

AVMA. "Report Looks to Future of Veterinary Profession." *JAVMA News* (March 11, 2020). https://www.avma.org/education/tips-veterinary-jobseekers/new-hire-mentoring-programs.

AVMA. "Veterinary Telehealth: The Basics." Telemedicine & Telehealth in a Veterinary Practice. Accessed September 16, 2020. https://www.avma.org/resources-tools/practice-management/telehealth-telemedicine-veterinary-practice/veterinary-telehealth-basics.

Howard, Brendan. "Transparency and Unconditional Positive Regard in Veterinary Medicine." *DVM360*, October 29, 2019. https://www.dvm360.com/view/transparency-and-unconditional-positive-regard-veterinary-medicine.

Lester, Bob. "We Can't Afford to Wait." *Today's Veterinary Business*, February, 2020. https://todaysveterinarybusiness.com/consumers-wont-wait/.

McReynolds, Tony. "What Millennial Pet Owners Want." AAHA. October 2, 2019. https://www.aaha.org/publications/newstat/articles/2019-10/what-millennial-pet-owners-want/.

CHAPTER 11

Becker, Marty. "Fear Free Pet Visits – How to take the Pet Out of Petrified." *Fear Free, LLC,* January 14, 2016. https://fearfreepets.com/fear-free-pet-visits-how-to-take-the-pet-out-of-petrified/.

Martin, Debbie. "The Veterinary Technicians' Role in Implementing Fear Free." *Today's Veterinary Nurse*, (Summer 2017). https://todaysveterinarynurse.com/articles/the-veterinary-technicians-role-in-implementing-fear-free/.

"The Physiologic Effects of Fear." *DVM360*, August 1, 2014. https://www.dvm360.com/view/physiologic-effects-fear. Turner, Joey. "Dogs: Emotionally Intelligent as Teenagers." Global Animal. Accessed June 2, 2020. https://www.globalanimal.org/2018/01/12/dogs-moody-as-teenagers-smart-as-two-year-olds/40328/.

Tucci, Jacqueline. "5 Signs Your Dog Is Emotionally Intelligent." *World of Angus* (blog), October 23, 2016. https://blog.worldofangus.com/5-signs-your-dog-is-emotionally-intelligent/.

CHAPTER 12

Animal Intuition (blog). "Intuitive Connections with Animals." Accessed September 10, 2020. https://animal-intuition.com/intuitive-connections-with-animals/.

Ehrhorn, Emily. "Extreme Animal Cruelty Can Now Be Prosecuted as a Federal Crime." *The Humane Society of the United States*, November 25, 2019. https://www.humanesociety.org/news/extreme-animal-cruelty-can-now-be-prosecuted-federal-crime.

Melson, Gail F. and Audrey H. Fine. Handbook on Animal-Assisted Therapy: *Theoretical Foundations and Guidelines for Practice*. Amsterdam: Elsevier, 2010. https://www.sciencedirect.

com/topics/agricultural-and-biological-sciences/pet-ownership.

Prokop, Pavol and Christoph Randler. Ethnozoology: Animals in Our Lives. Amsterdam: Elsevier, 2018. https://www.sciencedirect.com/topics/agricultural-and-biological-sciences/pet-ownership.

"The Evolution of Pet Ownership." Pedigree. Accessed September 10, 2020. https://www.pedigree.com/dog-care/dog-facts/the-evolution-of-pet-ownership.

Weliver, David. "The Annual Cost of Pet Ownership: Can You Afford a Furry Friend?" *Money Under 30*, Modified July 7, 2020. https://www.moneyunder30.com/the-true-cost-of-pet-ownership.

Western Animal Clinic. "What Does Your Pet Mean to You?" December 19, 2017. https://westernanimalclinic.ca/what-does-your-pet-mean-to-you/#:~:text=Our%20pets%20bring%20more%20to,actions%20when%20owning%20a%20pet.&text=He%20points%20out%20that%20we,the%20unconditional%20love%20they%20provide.

CPSIA information can be obtained
at www.ICGtesting.com
Printed in the USA
LVHW020910250521
688399LV00004B/52/J